CHEATING DEATH

CHEATING

DEATH

The Promise and the Future Impact
of Trying to Live Forever

Marvin Cetron
and
Owen Davies

ST. MARTIN'S PRESS
NEW YORK

Design by Michael Mendelsohn

Library of Congress Cataloging-in-Publication Data

Cetron, Marvin J.
    Cheating death : the promise and the future impact of trying to live
forever / by Martin Cetron & Owen Davies.—1st ed.
        p.   cm.
    ISBN 0-312-18065-9
    1. Aged.   2. Gerontology.   3. Longevity.   4. Aged—Health and hygiene.
    5. Aging—Prevention.   I. Davies, Owen.   II. Title.
HQ1061.C367   1998   97-35510
305.26—dc21   CIP

First Edition: February 1998

10   9   8   7   6   5   4   3   2   1

This book is dedicated to our wives,

GLORIA *and* **JANICE**

—*the only women we know*

with whom we can imagine being happily married

for what may well approach a century.

ACKNOWLEDGMENTS

Though usually only the authors receive credit for their work on a book's jacket, any effort of this magnitude is by definition a group project. Many others have more than earned recognition for their roles in the preparation of *Cheating Death*. For their invaluable contributions, we owe deep thanks to the following people:

Val J. Halamandaris, President of the National Association for Home Care, who generously provided much of the data about home and hospice care that informs Chapter 4 and Appendix A.

Marilyn Dean, R.N., M.P.H., B.S.N., National Director of Health Care Services for Interim Healthcare, and Janet E. Neigh, Chief Executive Officer of the National Association for Home Care, for their illuminating views into the future of home care.

Courtney Campbell, of the University of Oregon, in Corvallis; Ronald A. Carson, Chairman of the Institute for Medical Ethics at the University of Texas Medical Branch at Galveston; Rabbi Arnold G. Fink, of Beth El Hebrew Congregation, in Alexandria, Virginia; Monsignor Robert Paul Mohan, Professor Emeritus of Philosophy at the Catholic University of America, in Washington, D.C.; and Carol Taylor, C.S.F.N., of Holy Family College, in Philadelphia, who all supplied valuable insights into the ethical and religious implications of aging research.

Our friend Ken Dychtwald, whose continuing studies of the role of aging in America provided an invaluable foundation for our own analysis of recent developments in geriatric science.

Susan Cohen and Richard Morin, whose work for *The Washington Post* forms the basis of Appendix D.

The entire staff at St. Martin's Press, whose many labors on behalf of *Cheating Death* have been crucial at every step of the project.

And above all George Witte, our editor and friend, without whose insight, skill, and sheer hard work this book would never have been begun, much less completed. Thank you, George.

—MARVIN CETRON and OWEN DAVIES
June 1997

CONTENTS

FOREWORD

In 1980, Alvin Toffler published *The Third Wave*. In retrospect, it seems both a watershed event and a case study in failure. Toffler was not the first pundit to understand the transforming power of the computer; Forecasting International had examined the subject in business and academic reports for most of a decade, and we were far from alone in this. Neither was Toffler the last to deal with the rise of the information-based society that now is crystallizing all around us; in 1982, both *Encounters with the Future* (by Marvin Cetron and Thomas O'Toole) and John Naisbitt's *Megatrends* considered the subject. Since then a minor industry has grown up to dissect, explain, and predict the social and economic impact of computers. Yet *The Third Wave* marked a turning point. It spent months on the *New York Times* best-seller list. It was read by hundreds of thousands of Americans and similar numbers in other lands. After Toffler's work appeared, no literate, thinking person could claim to have been entirely unwarned of what was to come.

It did remarkably little good. Over most of two decades, the revolution has progressed much as Toffler foresaw. Desktop computers have spread throughout the developed world, changing both our working lives and our leisure activities. The Internet has grown from a tiny experiment by the U.S. Department of Defense to a global force for change. Whole new industries have been born, while jobs have been wrung wholesale from older, less productive fields. And in spite of Toffler's efforts, and ours, and those of other forecasters, these developments took most people by surprise. Warned that dramatic changes were coming, told clearly that many of their former occupations were obsolete, nonetheless they plodded forward into the path of an economic steamroller. Given the information they needed to cushion their lives against disruption, they arrived in the present unprepared. It has been thus ever since Apollo gave Cassandra the power of prophecy, but decreed that she would never be believed.

Still, we hope that this time will be different. There is another revolution coming, a development so remarkable that even among the forecasting community few have yet taken it seriously. We will simply state our premise here and leave our evidence for Chapter 1.

Science has at last begun to understand the fundamental processes of aging. As a result, it soon will develop ways to keep us from growing old. The human life span today amounts to only 75 or 80 years, on average, in the developed nations. Soon it will be much longer. Today's adults may well live to between 110 and 120 years, retaining all the health and energy of midlife. It is at least possible that they will live much longer than even we now expect, on into the unguessable future. This revolution may be the most important change that humanity ever undergoes.

We will deal with the science of life extension briefly, by way of preparation, for the claim that we soon will gain something approaching immortality requires firm support if it is to be taken seriously. However, once that case has been made, this book will move on to our real subject, the impact of this profound and unexpected development. Our concern is not for the far future, but for the next few decades, for the individuals and societies who are about to find that all their plans and expectations are obsolete.

The transition to a postmortal world will not be easy. As individuals and as nations, everything we do and believe is premised on the brevity of personal existence. Extend life even for a decade or two, and many things change. Prolong it indefinitely, and we transform human experience almost beyond recognition.

We will not even attempt to predict the details of a world in which mortality no longer seems inevitable. That task is too big for any single book, and the prospects of success at this early stage are too small. Instead, we will focus on a few crucial topics that are destined to shape our transition to the postmortal age. Medicine obviously is one, but religion, economics, government policy, and our changing values all will be equally important. Chapter 2 offers a brief survey of material to come. In this, we introduce the major subjects that concern us—the economic, political, and social structures that life extension is about to overturn. The next three chapters examine many of these subjects in greater depth. Chapter 3 considers Social Security, pension plans, Medicare, politics, and other practical aspects of American society that will be affected most immediately by any great change in our life expectancy. Chapter 4 looks at the vast medical industry, much of which may be rendered instantly obsolete. Chapter 5 extends these concerns to the rest of the world, where the diversity of cultures, economies, and social conditions greatly complicates any possible forecast.

The book's third section concentrates on the personal. In Chapter 6, we attempt to answer the obvious question "How can I prepare for a future so open-ended, so different from anything I ever expected?" Chapter 7 deals with the religious and ethical issues that life extension will raise. These are matters that soon must concern us all.

All these chapters deal with the first-order impacts of life extension, the direct effects of this abrupt change in the terms of our existence. Many other consequences will arrive at second and third hand, but will be no less important for being indirect. Our afterword considers five of the most significant and pressing.

Finally, our appendices offer background material. Some of it is related to life extension only indirectly. Yet it all helps to shape the context within which we will have to weather this difficult transition.

Appendix A considers an important aspect of modern health care, the home-care and hospice industries. We include them, not for the distant future, but for the next ten or fifteen years. During this intermediate period, the elderly will continue to sicken and die. The middle-aged, unless they can recognize and seize upon developments in life extension as they appear in the world's laboratories, will continue to grow old. For this near future, we still will need the help of doctors and nurses, not to avoid aging, but to deal with its effects, and we will have to obtain that help as efficiently and cheaply as possible. In many cases, that will mean learning about home and hospice care. We hope this discussion will provide a useful place to begin.

Appendices B and C offer the broadest possible look at the years to come. Over several decades of research, Forecasting International has recognized many forces that are molding the present into a much different future. In this most recent version, we identify seventy-four trends at work in the United States and fifty that apply to the world at large. Some are independent of life extension; computer technology, for example, will continue to advance whatever happens to our life span. Others are intimately related to aging research. We have tried to account for these differences in this revision.

With all its subtopics and appendices, this remains a brief book, not a vast and scholarly tome. It is not meant as a definitive analysis, but as an early warning. We often deal here with possibilities and portents, with implications rather than hard facts. But they are implications of enormous importance.

Science has occasionally followed promising leads and found itself at a dead end. Conceivably, the recent advances in aging research could prove to be another such time. Yet the evidence for a pending breakthrough is much more solid than even many scientists yet recognize. Forty years from now, we are more likely to live in a world of healthy, vigorous centenarians than we are to have grown traditionally "old" ourselves. This is a possibility we cannot afford to ignore.

Over the last twenty years, most of us have survived the computer revolution with varying degrees of discomfort. This time it may not be so easy. We hope that *Cheating Death* will give you both the time and the incentive to prepare for a life that should be longer, richer, and more challenging than any of us could possibly have expected.

CHAPTER ONE

THE COMING TRIUMPH OVER AGING

A ll right, we admit it. Not even the most optimistic of scientists expect to live forever. The world will not soon be "postmortal" in the sense that science will abolish death. But our exaggeration is much smaller than you probably assume.

The most profound transformation in history, the most fundamental change that humanity ever will experience, is as near as next week. It may already have begun. From this decade onward, the years of our lives will not be threescore and ten, but far longer. The Baby Boom generation, and perhaps its parents, can expect to live healthy, active lives that stretch to between 110 and 120 years. It is even possible that some of us may never die, save by accident or choice. Medicine, government, economics, religion—no single facet of human existence will remain the same.

PROMISES OF REVOLUTION

In the summer of 1995, several popular books told readers of a remarkable advance in the study of aging. A hormone called melatonin, they proclaimed, might have the power to hold time itself at bay. Mice receiving this natural, harmless substance survived to the human equivalent of 115 years. To the end of their very long lives, they retained all the health and vigor of youth. Just conceivably, people who used melatonin also might live far beyond their allotted span without ever growing old.

A furor greeted this announcement. Scientists debated the hormone's effects and squabbled about who deserved credit for the discovery of its age-fighting power. Doctors warned that melatonin might cause unknown harm. Skeptics denied that the results of experiments in mice could be applied to human beings. And in the United States, where melatonin is readily available, tens of thousands of ordinary people began to use this latest miracle drug. Some merely wanted a good night's sleep, for melatonin is a powerful sedative. Many others dreamed of taking a first step toward immortality.

Yet amid the hope and controversy, the true significance of this research was overlooked. What matters is not whether melatonin itself extends human life. It may well not. But discoveries related to melatonin have given scientists their first handle on aging. For decades, they struggled to figure out why we grow old. Now they can concentrate on developing a cure. And because the cause of aging has turned out to be relatively simple—a pinpoint failure in one biological system, rather than a general "wearing out"—a successful treatment should be much easier to find than, for example, the proverbial cure for cancer. Even if melatonin itself is not the final answer, it has become reasonable to believe that a practical remedy for aging is not far off.

This presents important problems. As individuals, we must plan for the forty years of added life that we suddenly can expect. As a nation, we must figure out how to support extra generations of healthy, vigorous, but chronologically ancient people who have no established role in society. As a world, we must find ways to share the benefits of aging research without undermining less flexible cultures or overcrowding our fragile planet. These and many other challenges could require answers in the next five years and almost surely will demand them in less than twenty.

In the pages that follow, we will seek to understand how the world must change when aging and death are no longer the ultimate facts of life.

SCIENTIFIC BACKGROUND

As a technical problem, aging is one of the most complex and elusive phenomena that scientists have ever studied. As early as

World War I, the Nobel Prize–winning physician Alexis Carrel observed that the wounds of older patients healed more slowly than those of the young. In the following years, he and his colleague P. Lecomte du Nouy discovered that some element in blood plasma caused the difference. Yet whether healing was promoted by a factor in the blood of the young or delayed by something in the blood of the old, they never were able to learn. It was the first of many such puzzles.

A few years later, Clive McCay of Cornell University found that putting rats on a diet that was nutritious but so low in calories that it could barely sustain life dramatically extended their survival. In one typical study, rats that ordinarily live for only 600 days survived to an average age of 1,100 days and some reached 1,800 days. Hundreds of scientists have confirmed this phenomenon in many different species. Mice, hamsters, and gerbils all live longer when calorie-restricted. Experiments with dogs and rhesus monkeys—much closer relatives of the human species—are not yet complete, but preliminary data suggest that calorie restriction will extend their lives as well.

These extreme diets confer other benefits as well. Mice and rats are prone to all the diseases that afflict aging men and women. However, when scientists cut their calorie intake by 30 to 50 percent, animals rarely become ill. Several years ago, scientists at Philadelphia's Institute for Cancer Research studied a kind of rat that always suffers from diseases of the heart, kidney, lung, and prostate, as well as several forms of cancer. When placed on a strict diet, only one animal in ten developed cancer. Just 2 percent suffered heart problems. None had kidney disease. Again, scientists have seen much the same reduction in disease in many different species.

In more than seventy years of careful work, no one has ever been able to explain how calorie restriction works its miracles. The trouble is that aging changes almost every aspect of the body's workings. Hormone levels, blood proteins, energy production, genetic activity—all these factors and many more vary with time, and there is no way to tell which might cause us to grow biologically "old" and which is merely an effect of aging. Scientists have proposed nearly fifty distinct theories to account for these observations. Experiments based on many of them have delayed the symptoms of aging, improved health, and extended the lives of laboratory animals.

Johann Björksten, a private researcher from Wisconsin, theorized that animals grew old because their proteins became damaged. He found that mice remained youthful when treated with enzymes that repaired the altered proteins.

Denham Harman, a biochemist at the University of Nebraska, suspected that aging stemmed from the effects of destructive chemicals known as free radicals. Drugs that combat free radicals also proved to slow aging.

Hematologist W. Donner Denkla, at the National Institutes of Health, believed that an unknown "death hormone" caused aging by shutting down energy production in the cell. To test this idea, he took aged rats and carefully removed their pituitary gland, the presumed source of the fatal hormone. Those animals too grew younger, lived longer, and rarely showed any sign of disease. "We never were able to identify the cause of death," Dr. Denkla once told us. "They appeared to be in perfect health right up to the end."

Other scientists have delayed aging in animals by reducing body temperature, by giving drugs to stabilize the cell membranes, by blocking the accumulation of waste products in the nerve cells, and by several other treatments. Each of these therapies was designed to test one theory of aging. None had any obvious connection with competing theories. Yet, in varying degrees, they all worked.

Although these results have puzzled biologists for decades, the explanation turns out to be simple. Almost all of these theories hold an element of truth, but each accounts for only a small part of the problem. Many of the changes wrought by time weaken the body and thereby promote further decay. Thus, preventing any of them slows the cumulative erosion that we know as growing old. However, all the early theories of aging—Björksten's protein damage, Harman's free radicals, and the rest—dealt with secondary factors. Hidden behind them, there lies a more fundamental source of aging.

This root cause has now been identified.

A CRUCIAL BREAKTHROUGH

By the mid-1980s, Dr. Walter Pierpaoli had already built a productive research career. Trained in both immunology and endocrinology, he had studied the immune system for nearly two decades. Along the way he had founded his own research center, the Institute for Integrative Biomedical Research, in Ebmatingen, Switzerland. For five years or so, he had grown increasingly interested in the role of an obscure hormone called melatonin.

Though little known then outside a small research community, melatonin already had proved to be remarkably versatile. In childhood, melatonin floods our bloodstream. When our supply wanes, we enter puberty. This is more than coincidence. Melatonin actively restrains sexual maturation until our bodies are well enough developed to support reproduction. Melatonin levels also vary on a daily cycle, rising in the evening and falling toward morning. We sleep and wake at the prompting of this inner clock. Later in life, we produce less melatonin, and the cycle becomes irregular. As a result, the elderly seldom sleep as long or as well as the young. In the 1980s, Dr. Pierpaoli and other scientists found that melatonin also bolsters our defenses against disease. As we grow old, we become more susceptible to illness largely because we no longer produce enough melatonin to keep the immune system operating at peak efficiency. The more people learned about melatonin, the more central its role in our lives appeared to be.

As he pondered what he knew about this hormone, Pierpaoli found an intriguing connection beginning to form in his mind. Melatonin seemed uniquely involved with time. It controlled maturation. It regulated our daily cycle. It was needed for many of the functions that decline as we grow old. Might it somehow govern aging itself?

He tested this notion by giving mice doses of melatonin each night, when their natural supply was at its peak. The animals lived much longer than normal. It was his public announcement of this discovery, in a *New York Times* best-seller titled *The Melatonin Miracle* (Simon & Schuster, 1995), that triggered the current wave of interest in this hormone.

However, subsequent studies proved even more revealing. This continuing research, though mentioned in his book, has gone relatively unnoticed.

On the basis of his work with the immune system, Pierpaoli concluded that the daily rise and fall in melatonin levels was more important to the body than the absolute quantity of the hormone. Therefore he tested the effects of giving melatonin during the day, when it would not restore the nightly hormone peak of older animals. This time his mice grew old and died on their natural schedule.

This was important, because it ruled out all the traditional explanations for aging. For example, if free radicals caused us to grow old, then melatonin should be even more effective when given during the day, because that is when free radicals are most abundant. Instead, it had no noticeable effect. So while it is true that melatonin inhibits free radicals, that appears to be just a coincidence; the inhibition has little or nothing to do with aging. This experiment ruled out all the other previous theories of aging for similar reasons. Timing, more than dosage, was what counted.

He then turned to the gland that manufactures melatonin. Known as the pineal, it is a small structure, about the size and shape of a kidney bean, located deep within the brain. Since the late 1980s, Pierpaoli and his colleagues have been transplanting pineals between mice.

At first, they simply took the pineals of young mice and implanted them in old animals, leaving the recipient's own gland in place. The aged animals lived a bit longer than mice treated with melatonin.

In the next experiments, they removed the pineals from old mice and replaced them with glands from young animals. This is an enormously delicate, stressful operation, and one-fourth of the mice died in surgery. Yet the survivors enjoyed longer lives than even melatonin could provide, the human equivalent of 125 years. (This suggests that while melatonin is important in aging, it is not the only substance whose loss contributes to growing old. Some other pineal factor, yet unidentified, may also be involved.)

Most recently, the scientists have tried swapping pineal glands between young and old mice. When young mice receive an old pineal, they die roughly when the aged donor would have done. When old mice receive a young pineal, they survive up to the equivalent of 140 years, or double their natural span.

Even if melatonin itself turns out not to extend human lives, the lessons from this painstaking work are clear. Aging begins in the pineal, with a specific change that disrupts the daily cycle of melatonin and perhaps other hormones. Now that scientists know where to look, they can find that change and prevent it, fix it, or compensate for it. If practical human life extension has not arrived already, it lies only a few years off.

There is a good chance that longer lives will bring better health. Like the animals in other longevity experiments, Dr. Pierpaoli's mice appear forever young and healthy, then die without warning or obvious cause. When science extends our own lives, we may no longer have to fear cancer, heart disease, emphysema, or the other disorders that now strike us down as we age.

There is one more implication here as well. If we live forty years longer than nature allows, we have four more decades in which science can extend our lives still further. Before today's adults reach 115 or 120, new treatments may well push death back to age 150, 200, or even into the indefinite future. Dr. Pierpaoli, for one, believes he knows where to find the next major advance in life-extending therapy. Unlike pineal transplants, it will be practical for human use.

And while we believe that Dr. Pierpaoli's work with the pineal offers the most promising insights into aging yet achieved, our expectation of a longer life does not depend on his continued success. In the thoughtful book, *Reversing Human Aging* (William Morrow, 1996), Dr. Michael Fossel, professor of clinical medicine at Michigan State University, argues convincingly that genetic engineering soon will prolong our lives far beyond their natural span. One way or another, practical life extension is nearly here.

The world ten or twenty years from now may not be literally postmortal. Yet our deaths are not likely to arrive on schedule. They might not arrive at all.

THE CULTURE OF MORTALITY

In our first chapter, we told of the remarkable change that suddenly is overtaking an unprepared world. The ultimate limit placed on us, either by a wise and benevolent Deity or by a mechanistic and uncaring nature, is about to fall. In times past, "old" has been almost a synonym for "decrepit," and great age has led inevitably to death. A decade or so hence, neither of these historical facts is likely to be true. If we are sufficiently attentive, the advancing years may conceivably bring us a trace of wisdom. They will not carry the infirmities that always have followed a scant few decades of life. Well into what would have been our retirement years, we will retain the health and vigor of people chronologically much younger. Death will still be decades off, and further research may well put it forward into the unguessable future. We will not be literally immortal, for we will remain vulnerable to accident and disease. Yet even today, given what we can foresee of science, we need no longer live in the expectation of sickness and death. This is the ultimate liberation.

Like all great liberations, the postmortal revolution will uproot much of what has gone before. In this case, the change affects the single most important fact of existence. Psychology, government, social expectations—almost everything we believe and do is based on the understanding that we will grow old and die on nature's schedule. When this ancient truth changes, we can expect dislocations on an epic scale.

We will devote the rest of this book to examining what the postmortal revolution will mean to us, both as individuals and as an increasingly global society. If we anticipate more than a tiny fraction of the changes to come, we will be well satisfied. We have been bred for one environment, have spent all our lives in it, and have built its assumptions into our marrow. Like the first fish that hauled itself out onto dry land, none of us is well prepared to foresee the new life that awaits us.

Before making our attempt, we should spend a few pages mapping the territory to be covered. Mortality shapes us, if not more than we know, then at least more than we usually care to consider. Each point at which it touches us represents a locus at which the world is about to change.

LIFE CYCLES

Sigmund Freud once wrote: "In our unconscious every one of us is convinced of his own immortality." Perhaps so. Yet in our conscious thoughts, only the youngest children are truly innocent of death. In youth, we face the loss of a pet or a favorite relative, and suddenly life is no longer the secure, unchanging place that well-meaning parents led us to believe it was. As adults, we see the sags and creases appearing in our mirrors each morning. The process is so gradual that we usually can ignore it. Yet none of us truly welcomes his or her fortieth birthday, nor any of the halfhearted celebrations that follow. Indeed, one reasonable test of adulthood is whether we have recognized and accepted the reality of our own impending death. It is an understanding that few of us escape for long, for the proof of time's dominion surrounds us.

Since life outgrew the single cell, existence has followed its immutable course. Morning becomes noon becomes night. Spring warms into summer, emerges into the bracing crispness of autumn, and fades into the bleak austerity of winter. Planting leads to harvest. Infants are born, grow to adulthood, coast for a time at the height of their powers, and then fall with increasing speed into the abyss. Life's schedule is inexact, and some hardy individuals are preserved to extraordinary ages. In classical Greece, when the average life span of men was only 22 years, Sophocles fathered a son in his 70s and wrote one of his greatest plays, *Oedipus at Colonus,* shortly before his death at the age of 90. Yet even the most durable of us gradually lose energy, fall prey to illness, and eventually die. Eternal youth is the stuff of myth, and immortality has been reserved for an afterlife the existence of which must be taken on faith.

Throughout history, that faith has been the cornerstone of life and society. It guides individuals. It shapes cultures. It informs religion in all its varied flavors. For at least 3,500 years, Hinduism has refuted death with its pantheon of gods and its cycle of reincarnation. Visions of the eternal Muslim paradise have inspired martyrs for fifteen centuries. (In fact, any rest for the Muslim soul may be brief. The Koran, in a clear argument for reincarnation, declares that "God generates beings and sends them back over and over again.") Even in the modern world of high technology, the assurance of resurrection and eternal life remains so compelling that in some surveys more than 40 percent of Americans say they consider themselves to have been "born again" into Christianity. Whatever form it takes, the underlying promise of all religion is that death is not final. Without that expectation, it has little to offer. In a remarkably prescient book, *The Immortalist* (Doubleday, 1969) writer Alan Harrington recounts a telling anecdote: "[The writer Miguel de] Unamuno suggested to a peasant that there might be a God in the form of a universal consciousness, but that man's soul might not be immortal. The peasant replied: 'Then wherefore God?' "

Harrington, proselytizing for a revolution against death almost thirty years before science made it possible, surveyed the numberless ways in which the fear of dissolution, the need to believe in our own permanence, shapes our beliefs and behavior. He found them wherever he looked. Our customs and deeds, he concluded, result from man's "disguised drive to make himself immortal and divine." We cling to our religious orthodoxies in hope of appeasing whatever angry deity has condemned us to die. Parents have children at least in part so that some aspect of themselves will survive after they are gone. Company presidents, demagoguing politicians, and stand-up comedians all build their power and celebrity in the subconscious hope of standing out from the crowd of lesser mortals and thereby qualifying for heavenly salvation. Suburban homeowners wash their cars and perfect their lawns in order to show off before the "computer of excellence," the nonsectarian ledger-keeper that Harrington believed had taken over the celestial recording authority of a God who in the late 1960s appeared to be dead Himself. Any effort to distinguish ourselves can, and probably should, be viewed at least in part as an attempt to gain admittance to eternal life.

What of all this will survive in a world where aging and death are no longer inevitable? Will religion still have something to offer people whose salvation is as near as the local pharmacy? Without the sword of death to compel us, will we lose all drive to achievement? Or will we find it possible to relax, to think more deeply and experience more fully, and in the end build more stable, rewarding, and productive lives when we need no longer fear that they will end almost before they have begun? This is one set of issues we must consider. There are others, some of them more immediate.

POCKETBOOK ISSUES

We are not only psychological but economic beings, linked by the complex networks of production and consumption. At least on average, our prosperity reflects the balance between the supply of goods available to us and the number of people among whom they must be shared. Given a stable population, as we produce more we become materially better off. But if population grows faster than production, our standard of living declines in proportion to the excess. Jobs help to keep production and consumption in balance. They ensure that people go to work where their productive capacity is needed, and they distribute the rewards of production to people who then use their wages to fund consumption. In the modern industrial economies, we divert a fraction of those wages, and of profits that might otherwise be apportioned as wages, to fund pensions and Social Security. These programs in turn allow us to remain consumers long after we have ceased to be active producers. In ways both obvious and subtle, this system is built on the assumption that we will grow old and die as we have always done. The decline of aging, and perhaps of death, will change its intertwined equations in many ways.

In the United States, Social Security already is in trouble. Contrary to popular belief, we do not live out our retirement years on the money that we and our employers contributed to the Social Security pension fund while we were still on the job. All that we put into the system is exhausted within a few years. Instead, we live on the contributions of those still in the workforce, as they in turn will exist on the generosity of workers yet unborn. This system functioned well at first, because relatively few people lived for more than a year or two after they became full-time consumers. Age 65 was chosen as the retirement age specifically for that reason. In the 1880s, when Otto von Bismarck established a pension system for employees of the German government, only one worker in twenty survived long enough to collect his first payment. In the 1930s, there were five American workers to support each retiree. Today, there are only two, and as medicine stretches our average life span the number continues to decline. By 2030, under current rules, the Social Security system will be bankrupt. Some estimates place the date as early as 2012.

Other countries face similar predicaments. Italy, saddled with what is widely regarded as the most unstable pension system in the world, is finding it difficult to support its retirees. Even in wealthy Japan, planners worry about how their retirement system will fare as modern health care has stretched life expectancies for the current generation to eighty years. In Russia, where simple bad planning bankrupted an entire country and voided the promise of lifelong support from the state, we see where the instability of social security programs could lead. Pensions seldom are enough to pay for a small apartment, utilities, and a livable diet. Often, pensions do not arrive at all. In any city, hungry retirees can be seen at informal bazaars trying to sell handicrafts, surplus furniture, even their old clothes in order to buy food. Throughout much of the developed world, the elderly could face a future as bleak as Russia's present if they must depend on government pensions to support their old age.

Life extension can only make the prospect of retirement more daunting still. No social security program in the world, and few private pension plans, can provide for the needs of pure consumers who can expect to live to the age of 115 or 120. We find it difficult to envision any traditional system of retirement that could cope with lives so prolonged as those the Baby Boom generation and its heirs are likely to enjoy.

Almost inevitably, this means that Baby Boomers are unlikely to retire at age 65. They may never be able to retire completely. Instead, they will remain in the job market or, if the anti-aging revolution is delayed slightly longer than we expect, will return to it. They will compete for jobs with younger workers, and by remaining in place for years beyond their original time of retirement, they will make it difficult or impossible for their successors to move from entry-level jobs into positions of authority. Suddenly, the effective number of workers will grow much faster than production. If, as we expect, the early twenty-first century is a time of general prosperity, the availability of extra workers may actually stimulate the growth of the economy. But, for a time at least, real wages will decline, while unemployment may well spike.

Certain businesses will be particularly affected by the transition to extended life. For example, the longer people remain healthy and active, the larger the market for sports equipment and clothing. And if older people can make do with part-time employment, many of them are likely to travel, bringing new growth to the hospitality industry. On the other hand, how many people will feel the need for life and health insurance if they can expect to live far beyond their natural span with little fear of major illness?

Life extension will transform one industry above all: health care. In the late 1990s, hospitals, clinics, medical laboratories, and related services represent fully 14 percent of the U.S. economy. Health care employs some 10.4 million Americans and pays out more than $283 billion per year in salaries. It is one of the fastest-growing industries in the national economy. As of 1994, the most recent year for which final results are available, health care grew by 12.5 percent, third in line behind space commerce (a much smaller industry) and data processing and electronic information services. This remarkable growth is expected to continue, thanks in large part to the fact that people are now living longer, into the years when they become subject to chronic illness and require more care.

It is not to be. Fully half of the money now devoted to health care in the United States is spent during the last six months of the patient's life, combating illnesses that doctor and victim alike know will prove terminal. And as we have seen in the previous chapter, any final decline almost surely will be compressed from months or years to weeks. Very possibly, we will simply pass out of life without warning or obvious cause, in good health to the last. We will continue to suffer broken legs, colds, auto accidents, and life's other random afflictions. Hereditary diseases will take their toll, at least until genetic research eliminates them. But these will not make up for the loss of heart disease, cancer, diabetes, arthritis, and the many other "markets" for health care that could all but disappear with successful anti-aging therapy. Hundreds of thousands of health-related jobs now expected to appear in the coming decades will never arrive. Hundreds of thousands of the jobs that now exist could vanish in the next fifteen years. The effects will ripple throughout the economy. Unemployment will rise. Wages will fall. Canada, Europe, and Japan face much the same economic shock. Thus growth will slow around the world. It could be many years before the global economy expands enough to give its unexpectedly large population the standard of living it once enjoyed.

POLITICAL FALLOUT

The United States once prided itself on being a "melting pot." It was, proud Americans told themselves, a place where people came from all over the world to build a better life. The best and brightest—artists, musicians, and more recently scientists—often found immediate acceptance, while others could start again. New immigrants could readily find jobs or form their own small businesses, learn English, and make a home in a land where all were free and equal, no matter their origins. Their sons, and even their daughters, could get a good education, and where their parents had been shopkeepers and factory workers, this second generation could become doctors and lawyers. Grandchildren could hope to become senators and congressmen, even presidents, their assimilation complete. Thus old identities were slowly abandoned by people who had found a better life. The foreign evils of ethnic hatred, religious intolerance, and poverty were washed away by the universal solvent of freedom. With hard work and time, all could become Americans.

This happy delusion ignored any number of inequities faced by those who sought acceptance in the new world. Too many of those tired and hungry yearning to breathe free found themselves in sweatshops and tenements, struggling with an urban American poverty no less oppressive than the agrarian variety they had fled in Europe. Political influence restricted economic benefits to the largely white, Anglo-Saxon Protestants who had arrived generations earlier. Irish and Italian immigrants struggled for decades to build their own political machines, which then acted to shut later immigrants out of the system, just as they had been excluded. And, of course, the inexcusable failure to possess white skin forbade assimilation and made economic progress difficult or impossible.

Yet like all good myths, the melting pot held a substantial element of truth. If assimilation was slower, less complete, and more painful than generally admitted, nonetheless it did take place. Italians and Irish, Poles and Czechs, Japanese and Chinese, Catholics and Jews might congregate in their own neighborhoods, practice their hereditary religions, retain a faded allegiance to their ancestral homelands. Still, after a few generations they all worked together well enough to perpetuate America's hands-on version of democracy and its idiosyncratically mixed culture. If blacks were left out, they usually were quiet enough to be ignored, and the nature of any heap is that someone always winds up on the bottom. Not even the American Dream could escape that law of nature—or so most Caucasian Americans could tell themselves.

The latest generations have traded in the old melting pot for a salad bowl. The accepted metaphor today is that Americans are like the components of a salad, each retaining its identity, but each contributing to an harmonious whole. If this image loses something from the dream of national unity and a unique American identity, it gains a great deal in its recognition of our remaining differences.

At a practical level, this change has fostered the growth of ethnic politics. African-Americans, Hispanics, Asians, Muslims, and a host of smaller ethnic and cultural groups have built political organizations to campaign for their legal and economic interests. The backroom horse-trading among leaders of the old WASP and Irish and Italian machines has given way to multibloc negotiations on almost every issue, whether of local control or of national importance. The one remnant of the melting-pot tradition is that this transformation has occurred in relative peace, with none of the street violence and little of the visible hostility that confronted the Irish and Italian political awakenings, and every African-American political movement from Reconstruction through the 1960s.

Age enters this political equation because the birthrate among immigrants and nonwhites is much higher than among native Caucasians, the average age of minorities is significantly lower, their life expectancy is shorter, and their access to health care is more limited. Because of the difference in birthrates and the high rate of immigration into the United States, the nation's ethnic composition is changing rapidly. Blacks, Hispanics, and Asians made up only 17 percent of the U.S. population in 1990. By 2000, one-third of Americans will be nonwhite. By 2030, they will be the majority. Whites will become just one more minority group in the diverse American population.

Life extension will complicate this trend because the wealthy and well-educated will benefit from it first. The unfortunate reality is that even today, in American society this translates primarily to people of European ancestry. Thus, although the complexion of local politics is changing, most national leaders remain white. So do the vast majority of top business executives. With the advent of life extension, many of today's Caucasian oligarchs will remain in place for years or decades longer than even they now imagine.

For the United States, this represents a threat that could not exist in a less diverse society. Political and business leaders held over from the Baby Boom era will be increasingly out of touch with constituents and employees whom they little resemble. Yet they will block the rise to prominence of younger successors from other ethnic backgrounds, who will resent their continued presence on the scene. In this transitional period, the long, slow hardening of positions among opponents who could face each other for decades may revive the current debate over immigration, affirmative action, and related issues, but in a much more virulent form. It will be very easy to lose the uneasy cooperation that makes today's ethnic politics viable.

FAMILY MATTERS

Any trend that concentrates wealth in the hands of a minority increases social tension. Any trend that raises the number of job seekers faster than the economy creates new openings for them also proves divisive. As we have seen, life extension will do both. It will provoke tensions nowhere more effectively than between the generations.

Older people already own the greatest share of society's wealth, because they have had more time to amass it and because their political power has skewed laws in their favor. They also are the most likely to invest in stocks and bonds. Longer lives will allow them to gather in an even greater share of the nation's capital. This growing concentration of wealth among the well-to-do elderly implies an equal deprivation among the young and the poorer old.

The failure of Social Security, and probably of most private retirement plans, will force many Baby Boomers back into the job market or prevent them from retiring in the first place. Older, experienced workers will retain their highly paid executive jobs, leaving their children and grandchildren with little opportunity for advancement. At the same time, those who once retired will compete for ill-paid service jobs that formerly would have given the young a way into the employment market. (We already can see this trend in action at any Wal-Mart.) This conflict of generational interests has the potential to create a kind of class warfare between the age groups in America as divisive as racial strife has been. It will not pit father against son as bitterly as the American Civil War once tore families apart. Yet the angry desperation of life-extended oldsters forced back to work will clash against that of young people who see their present and futures being sacrificed for the sake of elders both too foolish to plan for century-long lives and too selfish to die on time. The daily battle for survival will be felt in families throughout the land for most of thirty years.

This will reinforce trends that we already see, and trends that we can easily foresee. Parents will live in one area of the country, children in another, grandchildren in still others, wherever work takes them. They will see each other rarely, save in medical emergencies. Aging Baby Boomers separated from their families will band together to form artificial families, giving each other the practical and emotional support that once would have come from bonds of birth and rearing. They will return to their 1960s roots, building a new kind of commune designed for extended life. Yet it will be difficult to replace the emotional ties that once sustained both individuals and families. The result could be a growing sense of alienation that many of us will find difficult to endure.

These and many other changes will sweep through the world in the next fifteen or twenty years. They will transform society. They will transform our lives. In the chapters to come, we will examine them in greater detail. Though we cannot hope to picture the postmortal world in all its aspects, we will derive at least a broad outline of this startling future. It will be enough to help us plan for the issues we are about to confront. We will be dealing with them for the rest of our very long lives.

CHAPTER THREE

SOCIAL INSECURITY

Y ou probably have heard this "factoid" before; it was the most-quoted poll statistic of 1994. That September, a nonprofit activist organization called Third Millennium surveyed members of the 18-to-34 age group. It found that nearly twice as many young adults believed in the existence of UFOs as believed that Social Security would still be available for them by the time they retired. The young are not alone in this doubt. In another poll that same year, 80 percent of working-age Americans said they were "not too confident" or "not at all confident" that Social Security would give them the benefits that today's pensioners receive.

We are not about to endorse the existence of alien spacecraft, but those pessimists may well have been right about Social Security. Retirement programs both public and private are in trouble. So are many of the other institutions on which we all depend. As we began to see in the last chapter, many aspects of society have evolved or been designed for an environment in which we all died off approximately on a schedule that now seems obsolete. Extend our lives to any significant degree, and these critical mechanisms will break down. For the next few decades, much of politics in the United States will center on age-dependent benefits that have been established during the century now ending. Somehow we must save them, replace them, or learn to do without them.

As a result, the Baby Boomers are not likely to be as comfortable in their old age as their parents have been. Their children are likely to be even less well off. Twenty-something members of "Generation X" know that already. And they know whom to blame for their coming deprivation. This too could enliven American politics and society in the early twenty-first century.

To understand why, let us begin by looking at what it will take just to meet our national commitments to the Boomers, given the 80-year life spans that modern medicine has led us to expect. After that, we can attempt to figure out how things will change when our lives suddenly begin to stretch by several extra decades. Looking only at our economic and political situation, rather than at the benefits of a longer and healthier existence, even the baseline scenario is horrifying.

TOMORROW'S FORGOTTEN DREAM

For some of us, it is a house in the sun, perhaps on a private golf course in Florida or Arizona. For others, it is simply the home we have known for decades, more comfortable when the mortgage has finally been paid off and we no longer have to leave for work before sunrise on cold winter mornings. Perhaps we look forward to a chance to travel or to pursue the hobbies for which we have never had enough time. "It," of course, is retirement, that time of rest and anticipated pleasure when work is behind us, our financial future is in order, and we can finally relax and enjoy the rewards earned through long years of labor. It is a dream that not everyone has been able to realize, even in the World War II generation, which has benefited from the best that Social Security, private pensions, and Medicare have had to offer. Yet those who reached age 65 in the last twenty years have enjoyed the most comfortable senior life that any generation yet born can hope to achieve.

That will come as a shock to the Baby Boomers. Nine out of ten of them say they want to retire at or before age 65. Some 60 percent of Boomers hope to end their careers before age 60! A bit more than two-thirds expect to live comfortably, wherever they want, throughout the fifteen or twenty years they plan to spend in retirement. No less than 71 percent of them expect to live as well as or better than they did while still on the job. It is not going to happen. Few Baby Boomers are likely to retire, or at least to remain retired, unless they can live on their own savings and investments. Anyone born after, say, 1965 is likely to work long into an extended old age.

If we rule out such opportunities as panhandling and relying on the generosity of relatives, there are only four ways people can support themselves beyond age 65. We can collect benefits from Social Security and Medicare, or the equivalent programs for government workers. We can collect benefits from a private pension. We can live on our personal savings and investments. Or we can keep working. Boomers have already rejected that last option. What of the others?

Most of us build our retirement plans around Social Security and Medicare. No one imagines that we can live comfortably on Social Security payments alone. Yet neither can most of us afford to do without them. It is true that some 40 percent of Social Security funds go to beneficiaries whose incomes are above the U.S. median, while somewhere between 600,000 and 800,000 millionaires receive Social Security payments each month. Yet without their government stipend, an estimated 54 percent of Social Security beneficiaries would be poor.

Unfortunately, the national retirement and medical-assistance programs represent promises that the United States cannot hope to make good, at least under current circumstances. Consider some basic facts:

- There are 76 million Baby Boomers, the largest generation in American history. By comparison, the World War II cohort that makes up the current crop of retirees was scarcely 50 million. The generation to follow, the children of the so-called baby bust whose taxes are supposed to support the Boomers in their retirement years, amounts to only 44 million people.
- Social Security now gives payments to some 26 million elderly. (Other recipients include 3 million children and 4 million disabled people.) There will be 40 million Americans of pensionable age by 2010, and their ranks will have only just begun to grow. The number of beneficiaries scheduled to collect Social Security payments will double by 2040, even without anti-aging therapies to magnify the late-life population.

- By far the fastest growth will occur in the oldest segment of the population. The number of Americans age 65 to 69 will roughly double in the next fifty years. During the same period, the number age 85 and older will triple or quadruple. Not only will they need far more medical care than younger people, roughly 2.5 times as much per capita under current assumptions, they will need a disproportionate amount of social services as well. Three-fourths of people in this age bracket are single, divorced, or widowed.

- Already, health care represents slightly more than 14 percent of the American economy. By 2005, it will consume 18 percent of the GDP, at least five times as much as we now expect to spend on defense. And that is fully ten years before the Baby Boom generation begins to approach its peak medical-spending years. By 2020, the national doctor's bill will be far higher. Medicare alone spent only 2.5 percent of the American GDP in 1994. By 2020, it will grow to 6 percent of the GDP.

- During this century, Americans have gained 28 years in life expectancy. The average Social Security recipient now receives payments for years longer than planners anticipated when the program was designed in the 1930s. And post-retirement life continues to stretch. To give to pensioners in 2030 the same average period of benefits that people used to receive, we would have to raise the retirement age from 65 to 74. Of course, this supposes that nothing between now and then will extend our life expectancy even further. And we know that is a bad bet.

- Social Security pensioners who retired in 1996 will, on average, receive in benefits every penny they paid into the system during their working lives in just 6.2 years. Those working for the minimum wage will recover the taxes they paid in only 4.4 years. The average one-earner couple who retired in 1996 will receive about $123,000 more in Social Security benefits than they and their employers paid into the system. Medicare adds another $127,000 to this little-recognized profit.

- According to demographers Ronald Lee, of the University of California at Berkeley, and Shripad Tuljapurkar, of Mountain View Research, each added year of life expectancy beyond retirement adds 0.8 percent to the lifetime per capita cost of Social Security payments.

All this adds up to rapid growth in spending on government benefits to the elderly. The Social Security program now takes in more money in taxes each year than it spends, and pensions are paid out of interest on the Social Security trust fund. By 2013, the cash will begin to run in the other direction, and some of those payments will have to come from principal. By 2030, when the youngest Baby Boomers reach their 66th birthdays, the Social Security trust fund will be bankrupt, and the program will be losing money at the rate of $766 billion per year. Medicare will be broke in the year 2002. By 2030, it will be losing fully $1 trillion per year. A decade later, the combined annual deficit will reach $3.2 trillion. By 2050, it will be $5.7 trillion.

Already, Social Security owes American adults nearly $9 billion more than the taxes they have paid into the system. This deficit amounts to $675 million per year. Medicare and the separate pension program for federal employees add another $1.8 billion to the annual shortfall. As soon as 2002, benefits to the elderly will eat up nearly half of all federal spending other than interest payments on the national debt; in 1965, it was just 17 percent. By 2025, according to the General Accounting Office, this spending will drive the federal budget deficit to more than 20 percent of the Gross Domestic Product, up from just 2 percent in 1994. The national debt, 53 percent of the GDP in 1994, will reach 200 percent of the GDP. Five years later, in 2030, every penny of the federal budget will be devoted to Social Security and Medicare; there will be nothing left for other programs.

That sounds bad enough as it stands. But if we translate it into individual terms, it gets much worse. Over their lifetimes, Americans born in 1900 have paid an average of 24 percent of their earnings as taxes. Children born in 1990 will end up paying a lifetime net tax rate of 37 percent. Future generations, the workers who will have to support Social Security and Medicare when all of the Baby Boomers have finally retired, will lose no less than 82 percent of their lifetime income to the tax man. Even the Republican budget proposals of 1996, which were widely condemned as "gutting" Social Security, would reduce the lifetime tax rate only to 72 percent of income.

It can't happen. The Baby Boomers will not have their idyllic retirements if they count on Social Security and Medicare to keep them going. These programs, at least in their current form, will not be there for any generation that is not already receiving benefits.

Yet to a remarkable extent, the Boomers do count on government support for their survival in later life. Their other options for retirement income—private pensions and savings and investments—are not much more promising than Social Security. And the Boomers have given them surprisingly little attention.

Outside government and the military, fewer than half of American workers are covered by pensions. Only 30 percent of companies even offer a pension plan, and their numbers are highest in the heavily unionized industries and large corporations—the sectors where "downsizing" has been eliminating jobs the fastest. Rather than remaining with a single company for the twenty or thirty years it takes to qualify for corporate retirement, Americans today are far more likely to switch jobs five or six times during their working years, to work at home, or to take part-time jobs. None of these career paths leads to a pension. (Current plans to make pensions portable from one company to another will ease the problems of workers who often change full-time jobs but will do nothing for part-time workers or the growing numbers of self-employed.) In any case, most company retirement plans are a lot less generous than most of us probably imagine. The average pension gives beneficiaries just one-third of their pre-retirement income, and that is before inflation starts eating away at it. In addition, many corporate retirement plans are inadequately funded. Although private pension arrangements in general are not in the sorry economic condition of Social Security, there is reason to wonder whether many workers will ever collect even the meager rewards their employer's benefits planners have led them to expect.

That leaves savings and investments to fall back on. Over the years, our national savings rate has been dropping rapidly. In the 1960s, Americans managed to bank 8.1 percent of the Gross Domestic Product. Over the next twenty years, that dropped to less than 4 percent. In the 1990s, the savings rate has fallen still further, to 2.3 percent. It is now the lowest of any major industrialized nation and continues to fall.

The typical Boomer does not have any savings at all. Despite the vast river of money that has flowed toward mutual funds throughout most of the 1990s, a survey by the Federal Reserve Board found that only three American families out of ten have managed to save anything at all for the future. Some 43 percent actually spent more than they earned, racking up consumer debt. Another study found that half of all U.S. families had less than $1,000 in assets. Even by their late fifties, most had accumulated less than $10,000. This will not fund anyone's retirement.

GOLD FOR THE GOLDEN YEARS

Lacking both pension and investments, Boomers in their senior years may have little choice but to forget retirement and stay on the job. This is not unprecedented. For a notion so hallowed, the concept that everyone is entitled to retire, much less to do so largely at government expense, is surprisingly new. At the dawn of the twentieth century, men labored for as long as they were physically able to do so. Decades later, little had changed. When Social Security was enacted in 1935, it was viewed less as a retirement program for the able-bodied than as a defense against poverty for those too old and sick to work. As late as 1950, an easy majority of 70-year-old men who retained their health kept their jobs as well. It was not until the World War II generation neared pension age that Social Security came to be seen as conferring an inalienable right to years of leisure. This may well prove to have been a temporary aberration in a world where lifelong labor is the rule.

There is a problem with this option as well, however. Even if Baby Boomers resign themselves to working through their senior years, it is not at all certain that there will be jobs enough to go around. Many companies force older workers to retire, if not by overt corporate policy then through the subtle pressures of ageism.

Thus it may well turn out that few pension-age Boomers can simply stay on in their old jobs. Most will find themselves looking for work just when they had hoped to be done with the daily grind, in an employment market where executives of 45 or 50 often are considered too old to hire. They may be welcome as sales clerks or in other unskilled roles. American business culture has a good deal of adjusting to do before retirement-age Boomers will find it easy to step from one senior position to another.

Neither is it clear that they will be equipped for whatever well-paid jobs can be had in the early twenty-first century. The generation born after World War II is the last for whom factory work seemed to offer steady employment, the last to work in many-layered corporate hierarchies that promised frequent opportunities for promotion, the last to earn the high salaries possible in an economy dominated by unions and largely insulated from less well paid foreign competitors, the last to grow up without computers. Their world is quickly vanishing. In the 1970s and '80s, factory automation wiped out most of the assembly-line jobs that once promised high school graduates a middle-class income. In the 1980s and '90s, downsizing is cutting white-collar jobs just as quickly and almost as completely. Over the next few years, most of the surviving factory jobs and many of the remaining middle-level executive positions will disappear. Many of the factory workers and executives whose jobs evaporate will lose their careers as well. The average downsized executive takes a pay cut of one-third, even when it is possible to remain in the same industry or the same sort of job. Many older workers have been forced to retire, unable to find positions comparable to the ones they knew and unable to qualify for those that can be had in the '90s. The situation can only be worse for Boomers who find themselves beached in the early 2000s.

At regular intervals, the Bureau of Labor Statistics forecasts trends in the labor market for the next ten to fifteen years. The most recent of these reports carries us only to 2005. Yet it offers some useful insights into the work environment that retirement-age Boomers will confront a decade later.

One key factor in employment projections is growth in the adult population. The faster the U.S. population expands, the more demand there will be for goods and services and the more jobs will be created to serve that market. Between 1990 and 2005, the United States will add some 30 million people aged 16 and over. This is significantly fewer than in the previous fifteen years, and growth is expected to remain relatively slow throughout the early twenty-first century. There simply have not been enough children born to mature into consuming adults during the next few years, and there is little prospect that birth rates will rise in the near future.

In 1990, total employment in the United States was 122.6 million. By 2005, that should reach 147.2 million, an increase of 24.6 million new jobs. This is little more than half of the growth seen in the previous fifteen years.

The number of people competing for those jobs will grow as well, from 125 million to 151 million. This increase, 21 percent, is also off from the pace of recent years. Yet it represents 1.4 million more new job seekers than new openings for them.

What kind of jobs will be available? The U.S. economy is partway through a continuing shift from manufacturing to service industries. Services accounted for 38 million jobs in 1990. By 2005, they will provide 50.5 million openings, or 12.5 million new jobs. This makes services easily the fastest growing segment of the economy. It also represents nearly half of all the new jobs that will appear during this period. By 2015, we expect the service industries to generate an even larger portion of the new jobs that become available.

Unfortunately, services in general provide just two kinds of employment: poorly paid, mostly dead-end jobs for unskilled workers; and well-paid positions that require a good deal of specialized training. In this environment, late-life Boomers could easily find that the only jobs for which they are qualified are the ones they do not want, the jobs that will not pay a living wage.

The two largest industries in this sector are health care and business services. They also are among the fastest growing. Health care employment will expand from 8.9 million to 12.8 million between 1990 and 2005. Home health care, the single most rapidly expanding industry in the economy, nursing homes, and medical office staff all will demand hundreds of thousands of new personnel. So will computer and data-processing services.

In both these industries, we see the dilemma that eventually will face middle-aged Boomers who may be desperate for a new career. Health-care employers will pay well for qualified nurses and medical technicians, but only poorly for nurse's aides and orderlies, for whom there will be many more openings. Top programmers will command good salaries, but many openings will be for poorly paid data-entry personnel, who will be in even greater demand. And in business services particularly, the greatest demand, but the least security, will come from temporary help agencies. Boomers who lack the right backgrounds will have either to get new training, almost surely at their own expense, or to take whatever jobs are open to the unskilled.

School enrollments are rising at the moment, so there is a healthy demand for teachers and administrators at all levels from elementary school through college. The return of seniors for job retraining and part-time education will add to this need. Between 1990 and 2005, education will grow from 9.4 million jobs to 11.7 million, or 24 percent. Many of these positions will be desirable, because state and local school boards have reluctantly come to realize that if they want good teachers they must be willing to pay for them. But anyone who wishes to become a teacher will have to return to school for pedagogical training and certification. Displaced Boomers will not find this field a quick route to economic survival.

Other fields are growing as well. Social services; finance, insurance, and real estate; and transportation, communications, and public utilities all will have their "Help Wanted" signs out in the next few years. But they do not provide the plentiful opportunities to be found in more populous industries.

Job seekers who need employment fast between now and 2005 will have to look in the largest, and generally least-well-paid, employment sector, retail and wholesale trade. These areas will grow by only 26 percent and 16 percent, respectively, but because they are so large they will generate a total of 6.1 million new openings over the fifteen years covered by the study. To date, former executives and factory workers have not found that becoming a sales or stock clerk at a dollar or two per hour more than the minimum wage makes up for the loss of their previous jobs.

This is very much the work environment in which retiring Baby Boomers will find themselves in 2010 and beyond. In the aftermath of downsizing, the American economy, increasingly exposed to competition from abroad, is unlikely to offer as many well-paid jobs as it did when they were building their first careers. Those jobs that provide a living wage will require specialized training that only a minority of Boomers will possess. Whatever jobs can be had without that training will not pay for the comfortable lifestyles that today's 40- and 50-year-olds envision for themselves. Save for those few who are blessed with good pensions or adequate savings, Boomers are likely to find their "golden years" unexpectedly bleak.

THE REAL TWENTY-FIRST CENTURY

Of course, all this represents the consensus future, the one in which Boomers grow old and die on Nature's schedule, as modified by conventional medicine. In some ways, this least-likely scenario is the best the future has to offer. If people were all to grow old and die as we once anticipated, it would spare us many economic and social challenges that seem destined to bedevil society for many decades to come. What will happen in a world where more than 75 million people have the unexpected chance to live far beyond their allotted span? How many superannuated Boomers will survive to collect Social Security for three or four decades longer than their parents did? How many of them will be able to survive on their own pensions and savings? How many will remain in the workforce, competing for jobs with their own descendants? How many suitable jobs will be available for those who need them?

At this point, we reluctantly step from the familiar, disciplined world of forecasting into the treacherously borderless realm of speculation. We simply do not know how soon the anti-aging experiments now being carried out successfully in mice and rats will yield therapies suitable for human use. Neither can we forecast how quickly survival-minded Boomers will adopt these treatments once they become available. To make any tentative forecasts at all, we will have to pick dates that sound "reasonable" to us, insecure in the knowledge that we probably will prove to have guessed wrong.

Still, the animal experiments have been very clear in their implications for human aging. They are not like cancer research, with its million possible lines of study. Instead, Dr. Pierpaoli's transplants of the pineal gland are like discovering that your ancient, balky automobile suddenly runs well if you replace its old carburetor with a new one, while a neighbor's new car coughs and wheezes when given your old carburetor. You may not know exactly what is wrong with the carb, but there is not much doubt where the problem lies. Given this kind of hint about the nature of aging, it should not take scientists long to find a workable cure. For the sake of argument, let us say that researchers will need ten years, beginning in 1996, when Dr. Pierpaoli's work gained widespread publicity. We know that fifteen years probably is just as likely, while twenty years is not out of the question.

How long will it take senescent Boomers to adopt whatever anti-aging therapy eventually emerges from this research? If the response to earlier promises of better health is any indication, not long at all. A year after the news breaks, several million people will have jumped onto this particular bandwagon. Five years later, after it has become clear that they are healthier, more energetic, more youthful in appearance—"younger," in fact—than their peers, the vast majority of their generation will join them. Only a few zealots convinced that life extension violates natural law in a way unacceptable to their Deity will reject any treatment proved to offer them extra decades of healthy existence.

However, by our target date of 2011—neatly, this works out to be the year in which the oldest Boomers turn 65—some people will have died or fallen irredeemably ill, while the number who reject treatment could be larger than we imagine. Let us say that 50 million members of the 1960s generation will choose to remain with us for an unnaturally long time. Somewhat more might be possible, considerably fewer would be entirely believable. In any case, they will be more than enough to change the baseline forecast beyond recognition.

So, in the real future, counting only this first life-extended generation, the United States alone will be home to some 50 million more people than planners now expect. Based on animal experiments, the oldest Boomers will remain with us through the year 2063, perhaps as late as 2068, while the youngest will survive until at least 2080. By then, their children will have been using anti-aging treatments for more than half a century, so the total population from roughly 2040 onward will be even larger than our back-of-the-envelope estimate would lead us to believe.

Note that even this startling change presupposes that there will be no significant extension of life beyond the one promised by current research. In fact, it seems much more likely that some time in the next half century a breakthrough yet unforeseen will push the end of life still further into the unguessable future. The population will be larger still.

One factor that does not change in this new reality is how few Boomers are prepared to retire on their own resources. Most will remain in the job market long beyond their nominal retirement date. Most of the rest will be forced back to work when it becomes clear that their savings cannot last as long as they will. Their children, of course, will never retire at all. So by 2020, at least 50 million people who expected to spend their later lives in pleasurable leisure will instead be scrambling for jobs. And most will be unqualified to earn a decent living in a world increasingly dominated by technologies they have only half-learned to use.

It would be easy to spin this out into a kind of Doomsday scenario, with hungry—but well-preserved—former hippies and yuppies huddled around trash-can fires in the ruins of New York and Chicago and Los Angeles, the economy growing too slowly to support their numbers, the beloved American Dream permanently collapsed under the weight of overpopulation, the generations fighting over what little hope and prosperity are left. We are not so pessimistic. Life extension will bring with it challenges that almost—but not quite—outweigh its promise. Yet we believe that society in general, and most of us as individuals, will cope with them successfully. We may eventually look back on the years from 2010 through 2025 or so as a time of enormous difficulty, when our economy, culture, and personal lives were transformed almost beyond recognition. Yet we will know that they gave us the only possible transition to a new and better life.

A DIFFICULT TIME

We are about to undergo a kind of forced evolution, both as a society and in our personal lives. It will be driven by the high pressures both to survive now that science has (almost) made it possible to do so and to earn a living when confronted with the evaporation of the comfortable retirement we always expected. Though the details of this process remain obscure, a few essential features are obvious even ten or twenty years in advance.

Whatever hope remains for Social Security and Medicare in these last few years before the Baby Boom reaches its traditional retirement age will be dashed by the advent of life extension. In a time when all can expect to live well beyond their centennial, no public retirement program can survive. Medicare benefits will be trimmed lightly at first, while co-payments will grow. Eventually, the program will be scaled back radically, save for those few remaining elderly for whom anti-aging therapies arrived too late. Fortunately, these treatments will so improve the health of the Baby Boom generation that Medicare will not be missed. Social Security is a different matter. Over strident protest, sometimes bordering on violence, the government will be forced to pare retirement benefits, even for those already receiving them. The retirement age will be pushed back from the 67 that Boomers now expect to 68, then 70, and finally 75. Eventually, it will become clear that even this is not late enough to provide an adequate living for people whose lives will stretch on for at least another four decades. Social Security will revert to its origins. It will become merely an insurance program for those whose health, despite all the medical advances to come, is too poor to permit continued work. This process will not be easy or immediate. Benefits for life-extended Boomers who already have retired will be reduced gradually over ten or fifteen years. But eventually people at any age will be expected to work for their living.

This means that, at least for a time, most of us will have to make do without the luxuries we have come to expect. We will not live in private houses or large apartments, but in small apartments or condominiums—whatever minimizes our outlay for shelter. By 2015 or 2020, few Boomers will have the resources to spare for more. They will be living on savings and investments that they know cannot last, or making do with ill-paid sales and service jobs while they struggle to find or create a more rewarding career.

Boomers of late have taken to calling themselves the "sandwich generation." Many find themselves struggling to help support both elderly parents and adult children. Even with Social Security and Medicare, their retired parents are saddled with incomes not much more generous than the Boomers' own will be two decades hence. Their children are finding it increasingly difficult to move out of the house, or remain out of it, in a high-tech economy where the work may be interesting but the salaries often are not. As a rule, their parents still live in their own homes, often in retirement communities in Florida or the Southwest. Yet three-generation households are increasingly common. This trend has been growing for the last decade. It will accelerate for years to come. In the not-so-long run, Boomers will take on their parents' role, moving in with children and grandchildren to share expenses.

Those who cannot will build new alternatives. Already, members of a few pioneering communities are sharing more of their lives than the back fence. In these carefully planned experiments, members have their own small houses or apartments, but often eat at a village cafeteria. They meet often to discuss mutual concerns, operate car pools, and enjoy homemade entertainment. Families trade off among themselves, sharing child-rearing duties so that children in effect have parents wherever they turn. House- and apartment-sharing have also boomed, especially among the young. Where one entry-level salary is too small to provide an independent living, two or three—or seven or eight—can support a group home with just enough privacy to be tolerable. In future, Boomers will adopt both these models. Many will build retirement-age, but not necessarily retirement, communities to minimize the inconveniences of life on a tight budget. Others will do as their children have done, sharing a house to stretch their resources. Ironically, the communes of the 1960s may be the old-age homes of the 2020s.

Other changes will do very little good if post-retirement Boomers cannot qualify for jobs capable of supporting them. Some will start their own companies. Others will find they can turn old hobbies into second careers as artists or craftspeople. Engineers, computer programmers, and the like may be able to update their skills and find jobs much like their old ones (though the half-life of an engineer's professional knowledge is only five years; anyone who has been out of the job market for long will have to start again, virtually from scratch). Some executives will cling to their old positions; we will return to this unwillingness to relinquish a job, for it will have unfortunate consequences. However, most Boomers will have to refit themselves for other roles. These new jobs will require technical training of a kind that relatively few Boomers have had to accept.

Thus the period from, say, 2005 to 2020 will be the time of re-education, when seniors who no longer are growing old refurbish themselves as computer programmers, technicians, designers, and skilled workers in technical trades we have not yet begun to imagine. The market for educators will rise even faster than forecast, largely to meet this urgent need. This will be a continuing process, for the pace of technological change is so fast—and still accelerating so fast—that most of the careers that tomorrow's seniors build for themselves will have to be replaced a decade or so later.

All this pressure—to abandon hope of retirement, to make do with a shrinking net income, to build a new career, to accept the open-ended promise of never growing old—will lead to another change as well. Under this unprecedented emotional stress, Boomers and their children will require a level of social and psychiatric care that American society has not yet been willing to provide. Until we grow accustomed to our new freedom from aging and our new responsibility to remain forever productive, we will urgently need whole armies of psychiatrists, psychologists, social workers, and other service professionals. Helping to meet that demand could give some would-have-been retirees a new role in life.

GENERATION WARS

This will be a difficult transition in other ways as well. In our baseline forecast, we found that there will be 1.4 million more new workers than new jobs during the period from 1990 to 2005. The picture looks the same for the years that follow, even in the ordinary course of events. The generation now reaching its early 20s is some 72 million strong, and demographers already are predicting that the children and teens of 2015, most of them yet unborn, will run to some 82 million. Job growth should accelerate as well. (In this forecast, we run counter to Social Security planners, who estimate that the economy will expand at an anemic rate of 2 percent per year for the next decade, eventually falling to 1.2 percent.) But jobs will not quite keep pace with the rapidly growing number of young people who need them. In the ordinary course of events, this would mean a modest drop in wages and a corresponding rise in unemployment.

But events in the next few decades will not be ordinary. Between 2012 and 2028, the Baby Boom generation was scheduled to leave the employment pool, making way for younger workers to pursue their careers. Given a longer life, some 50 million Boomers (in our roughest of all possible estimates) will remain in place. They will compete with their children and grandchildren for jobs that suddenly will appear very scarce indeed. Until the economy grows enough to supply work for this suddenly expanded labor pool, most people will find that making a decent living is far more difficult than ever. And it could take two or three decades to grow that many new jobs.

This could lead to all-out war between generations fighting for a share of scarce resources. Such a conflict would be easy to understand. Today's children and young adults can reasonably argue that their parents and grandparents have tilted the American economy in their own favor, at the expense of the generations that follow them. Social Security and especially Medicare are largely responsible for the growing national debt. These programs will benefit only those who reached adulthood during World War II, the Korean war, and the Vietnam war. Yet it will fall to "Generation X" and its children to pay their expenses. That task alone could easily undermine the benevolence that one generation might ordinarily be expected to feel toward its parents and grandparents.

Yet other stresses could be even more difficult to endure. Suddenly Boomers will be competing for jobs that their descendants expected to have to themselves. Executives and business leaders will cling to their positions long into extended old age. And each job filled by a Boomer is one that younger workers can view only with envy. Seniors who by rights should have retired years earlier will clog the flattened corporate hierarchies, making career advancement all but impossible for those less experienced. Under growing economic pressure, many of them will move back in to live with, or provide homes for, the very children whose jobs, and futures, they have taken. At work and at home, this intergenerational stress will be unremitting.

Many of these stresses will find expression in the public arena. Budget battles in Congress could center on such issues as who will pay off the national debt and how much public support should go to life-extended Boomers who reached old age without adequate nest eggs. A worst-case outcome could have ancient Boomers voting down school budgets and other benefits for the young, while their descendants take to the streets, protesting old-age pensions and job-training programs for the elderly, much as Boomers themselves once fought against racial prejudice and the Johnson administration's Vietnam policies.

Yet there are less troubling possibilities as well. How we resolve this potential conflict will depend not only on the state of the American economy and the willingness of Boomers to take responsibility for their own well-being in later life, but on attitudes of Generation Xers and the cohorts after them. Despite a Beavis-and-Butthead reputation, this baby-bust generation turns out to be remarkably literate and responsible. Though cynical about institutions, most Generation Xers are optimistic about their own ability to work hard and get ahead. Some 55 percent report being pessimistic about the nation's economy over the next decade, and more than half predict that it will be harder for them to own a home, build a business, or achieve financial security than it was for their parents. Yet half expect at middle age to live better than their parents did, while four out of five expect to bankroll their own retirements from personal savings. Remembering their own past as latchkey children, they plan to marry later—and to remain married.

Less is known about the children of the "baby boomlet," now

ending, and of course there is no evidence at all about the post-boomlet generation about to be born. The most interesting analysis of their potential that we have seen to date comes from William Strauss and Neil Howe, authors of *The Fourth Turning: An American Prophecy* (Broadway Books, 1997). They believe that history runs in cycles, each about the length of a long human life, and that each generation repeats the character of the generation that lived out the last similar role in history. Though we have a few reservations about the details of their vision, their basic insights into history and generational psychology seem sound.

According to Strauss and Howe, the United States will face a great social and financial crisis early in the next century. For a time, it will appear that the country has collapsed into a new depression, its economy and national cohesion both ruined beyond repair. Yet from this chaos a new social contract will emerge. Government will be streamlined and will shift its priorities from debt service and care for the elderly to public works and defense. Shared sacrifice will become the national watchword. Americans will accept that they can no longer expect retirement benefits and medical care from Washington and will take the responsibility for their own futures. For a time, society will become intolerant of crime, dissent, mental illness, and other deviations from the norm. Then some crisis will appear, a catalyst that will demand our national attention and promise that if only we can solve this one problem, all will be well. From this unpromising ground a new trust will grow—in our institutions, in each other, and in ourselves.

Well, perhaps. Certainly the recognition that current and future generations will live much longer than our ancestors did might well qualify as a catalyzing crisis, if one is needed.

However, what interests us is what Strauss and Howe have to say about the 13th Generation, as they call those born between 1961 and 1981, and the Millennials, born between 1982 and 2002. The authors compare these generations with their forebears some eighty years earlier, who lived at very similar periods of history. What they find is encouraging. In their view, the "13ers" are consummate survivors, bred with the skills required to clean up the debris left by earlier generations. Millennials are characterized by competence, courage, virtue, and a flair for teamwork. In the best of all possible futures, these two generations might just find the combination of strength and compassion required to forgive the Boomers their trespasses and rebuild society to accommodate lives that regularly outlast their century.

In truth, however, we have no idea how the potential age wars of the 2010s and 2020s will play themselves out. This period can only be a time of difficult adjustment until the United States has built an economy capable of supporting a much larger population and its citizens have grown accustomed to the idea of taking complete responsibility for their own well-being throughout a life span that few people have ever known. With foresight and goodwill, we can minimize the pain of this unprecedented transition. But foresight is one commodity never to be taken for granted.

CHAPTER FOUR

FAREWELL TO BIG MEDICINE

Almost by definition, being old means being frail. Though some people retain their health until very late in life, with time most of us become increasingly susceptible to diseases of all kinds. An estimated 80 percent of all deaths and 90 percent of all morbidity, as doctors call the symptoms and results of illness, stem from chronic diseases rather than colds, accidents, and other acute disorders. Medicine has banished most of the infections that once killed people early in life and in the process has stretched our life expectancy by 30 years. But instead of remaining healthy, we now succumb to cancer, heart disease, stroke, arthritis, diabetes, Alzheimer's, and all the other diseases that primarily afflict the elderly. Rather than being acutely ill for a short period, we suffer ailments that can stretch on for decades. By the age of 40, most people suffer from at least one chronic illness. By age 85, the average person must cope with no fewer than four separate disabilities.

This growing susceptibility to disease is so characteristic of later life that some scientists consider it the essence of the aging process. While we were preparing this book, one prominent researcher who has spent an active career studying the mechanisms of aging asked, "If an organism did not become more vulnerable to disease, how would you know that it was growing older?" A glance in the mirror suggests all too many casual replies, but it was a valid question. As we saw in Chapter 1, any therapy that stretches the lives of the healthiest animals also tends to delay or prevent whatever disorders usually afflict less fortunate members of the species. In many studies, life-extended animals remain healthy to the end of their lives and die without warning or obvious cause.

That raises an interesting possibility. If we really are on the edge of extending our own lives, health care as we know it could be nearly obsolete. In the life-extended future, we will still suffer from broken bones and other trauma. We will continue to get colds, influenza, and other infections. The unlucky among us will still be born with hereditary disorders, at least until modern genetics learns to prevent or cure these problems. But the great, unsolved infirmities of old age could begin to fade away.

This is important for reasons beyond the obvious improvement in our quality of life. Modern medicine is not just an elaborate tool for fighting disease. Throughout the developed world, health care is a major segment of the economy and an important source of employment. Much of this vast industry is devoted primarily to caring for the problems of the elderly. Hospitals, hospices, home-care agencies, medical laboratories, and the like will not disappear if humanity experiences a sudden, unexpected outbreak of good health. Yet the demand for many of their services may well contract sharply. Jobs will be lost, careers halted, hospitals closed or aborted in the planning.

A HANDLE ON HEALTH CARE

In this one book, we cannot hope to measure the total impact of the anti-aging revolution on the economic and employment prospects of the developed lands. Deriving any more than a rough qualitative idea of what to expect from this aspect of life extension will require detailed studies that could occupy teams of researchers for the next ten years—by which time the change may be almost upon us. However, we believe it is important to begin asking the right questions. How large is the health-care industry? How many of us does it employ? How many of those jobs depend on the frailty of old age? How many of them will be left if being old no longer means being sick? How will life extension change our personal health costs? How will it alter government spending and policy?

In this chapter, we hope at least to map out the territory that specialists will have to examine more fully. We will have to wade through some tedious statistics in the process, but please bear with us. The future of the health-care industry has implications for us all, even if anti-aging treatments prove so effective that we will rarely need care ourselves.

Fortunately, we already know a lot about the health-care industry. Among the nations of the Organization for Economic Co-operation and Development, health care represents between 8 percent and 14 percent of the Gross Domestic Product. In the United States, health-care spending totaled approximately $1 trillion in 1995, or 14 percent of the GDP. On a per capita basis, the United States spends more for health care than any other nation in the world. In 1995, we each spent, on average, more than $3,500 for health-related expenses, up from only $2,685 just five years before. Less than 10 percent of that goes to research, hospital construction, the administration of health programs, and other ancillary costs. More than 90 percent is spent directly on medical care.

By far the largest share of the nation's health budget goes for hospital bills. In 1994, the most recent year for which a final tally is available, 40.7 percent of total health spending paid for hospital care, some $386 billion. At that, hospitals were taking less of our health budget than in the past. In 1980, they absorbed about 47 percent of medical spending.

All that money represents jobs. In 1992, approximately 119 million Americans were employed. Of those, 8.5 million, or 7.1 percent, worked in the health-care industry. In 1993, the U.S. Bureau of the Census estimated that American health care involved nearly 472,000 separate businesses with 10.4 million employees and a total payroll of $283 billion per year—and those figures omitted government workers, the military, and the self-employed. Between 1982 and 1992, the American economy generated 17 million new jobs. Fully 2.7 million of those new openings, or 16 percent, were in health services.

In the consensus view, pre–life extension, that growth will continue throughout the foreseeable future. According to the U.S. Bureau of Labor Statistics, seven out of the fifteen fastest-growing jobs between 1994 and 2005 will be in health care. So will three of the ten fields that generate the most new jobs. (The two lists differ, because smaller fields can grow very rapidly, yet not create as many employment opportunities as a slower-growing but much more populous occupation.) The decade ending in 2005 will create new openings for 473,000 registered nurses, 428,000 home health aides, and 387,000 nursing aides, orderlies, and attendants. The fast-growing fields—such specialties as physical and corrective therapy assistants and aides, physical therapists, occupational therapists, and medical records technicians—will add another 1 million jobs during this period.

It is difficult to say how many of these new openings, or of the jobs that already exist, depend on the frailty of the elderly. Yet a few statistics make it clear just how much of disease, and therefore of health care, is related to aging.

In the United States, men have about a 50 percent chance of developing an invasive cancer at some point in their lives. A woman's chance is one in three. In 1991, a reasonably typical year, cancer killed just 9,000 people below the age of 35, but 354,800 above the age of 65.

Some 60 million Americans, one in four, suffer from some form of heart disease, high blood pressure, and related conditions. In 1991, 720,900 Americans died of heart disease. Only 5,300 were younger than age 35; 597,300 people succumbed during their retirement years. (Even this was a dramatic improvement over the historical toll. In 1950, no fewer than 424 people died of heart disease for every 100,000 population. By 1990, the death rate was down to 181 per 100,000.)

About 1.5 million Americans suffer a stroke each year, and 150,000 of them die. In 1991, strokes claimed only 1,400 people below the age of 35, but 14,400 in the next two decades of life, and 125,100 after 65.

Alzheimer's disease, of course, is unknown early in life. By the age of 80, one person in four shows evidence of this mysterious and deadly illness.

Not only are we more likely to become ill in old age, our symptoms, on average, will be more severe than those of a younger person. In 1991, pneumonia and influenza killed scarcely 5,000 Americans under age 55. Over age 75, no fewer than 58,700 died of infections that their bodies would have overcome with ease thirty years earlier.

A few spending figures also are conveniently available. According to one reasonable estimate, from age 30 to 34, the average man in the United States spends a bit more than $1,500 per year on health care. By the ages of 50 to 54, this has risen to nearly $4,500.

A number of studies have attempted to measure the economic value of therapies that primarily benefit the elderly. A 1994 report from the National Institutes of Health found that laser treatments for diabetic retinopathy, which can prevent blindness in up to 95 percent of the patients with this age-related condition, save between $1.2 billion and $1.6 billion per year, even though only half of the patients who need treatment actually receive it. (This estimate includes both medical costs and other societal expenses, such as Social Security benefits and lost tax revenues.) A study by the National Institute of Neurological Disorders and Stroke found that giving the anticlotting drug warfarin to patients with a form of irregular heartbeat known as atrial fibrillation could prevent 20,000 to 30,000 strokes per year, for a savings of $200 million. The savings could be even greater, as it has since been found that aspirin is just as effective as warfarin, and much cheaper. At these rates, diabetic retinopathy must still cost society at least $1.2 billion per year, not counting the price of laser surgery, while the 150,000 strokes that Americans suffer each year would incur about $1 billion more in direct medical costs. Chalk up about $2.2 billion that a successful anti-aging therapy might save from just two of the many disorders that usually strike elderly victims.

Medicare and Medicaid payments offer another window on health-care spending for the aged. According to preliminary estimates, Medicare's hospital insurance program covered 32,798,000 people of retirement age in 1996. Their average annual benefit was $3,327. Thus total spending for this one program was just less than $109.2 billion, all of which went to the aged. (We have omitted spending for the 4,730,000 disabled people who also received Medicare payments that year.) Enrollees in Medicare's voluntary program of supplementary medical insurance totaled 31,926,000 (again neglecting the disabled), with average annual benefits of $1,918. This comes to another $61.2 billion. Medicaid payments in 1994 reached approximately 4 million elderly people, who received an average of $8,243 each. Thus Medicaid payments added about $33 billion to government health benefits for the elderly. (This figure is stated in 1992 dollars. To make it strictly comparable to the Medicare estimate above, it should be raised by roughly 5 percent for inflation.) Thus, from these two programs alone, spending on health care for the aged totaled at least $203.4 billion. Payment figures for 1996 are not yet available, but would have been between 8 percent and 10 percent larger still.

That is not the full extent of the cost of caring for seniors, because Medicare pays only part of its beneficiaries' medical bills and often refuses to pay for home care and other necessary health expenses. In all, though Americans over age 65 make up only 13 percent of the population, most authorities hold that they account for one-third of spending on health care. That comes to about $340 billion per year as of 1996. Our back-of-the-envelope tally seems to confirm this estimate.

We have not yet sought out comparable data for the other developed countries, but would expect senior care to make up slightly less of their total health spending. Among all the major industrialized nations, only the United States has yet to enact a program of universal health care. In other lands, these plans have required the establishment of triage systems that either limit access to "heroic" life-saving measures for the elderly or require older patients to pay for their own treatment when expensive procedures are needed. In Great Britain, for example, anyone is free to obtain a kidney transplant, but older patients who need public funding can find themselves on waiting lists that stretch for years, while younger patients enter the line ahead of them. In some cases, the life-saving operation may be denied altogether. Elders who want immediate treatment must pay for it themselves. Despite these limitations, however, we would be surprised if care for older patients accounts for much less than 25 percent of all health spending in any of the developed countries. This still represents an important segment of each nation's economy and job market.

LOOKING AHEAD

In any baseline forecast—that is, one that neglects the promise of much longer, healthier lives—care for the elderly must absorb a growing share of our resources for many years to come. Inflation alone would ensure that. For the past four decades, the cost of health care has risen about 50 percent faster than the overall rate of inflation. In the ten years ending in 1992, for example, prices in general rose by 50 percent. Prices for health care rose by 110 percent. Inflation rates in general have slowed during the last few years, but the cost of health care continues to creep upward at something over 4 percent annually. This still is about half again the rate of inflation for the overall economy. At that rate, the nation's medical bills will grow by about 70 percent, or $1.75 trillion in today's dollars, by the year 2030.

New technology often takes the blame for raising the cost of health care. High-tech diagnostic and therapeutic methods, this argument goes, require enormous investments in equipment and trained, well-paid technicians to use them. Thus, both capital costs and above-average salaries must come from the payers' pockets.

One oft-cited example is CAT scanners, which can save the lives of a few desperate patients, but which until recently cost upward of $1 million per unit. In the early years of CAT scanning, it seems that many small hospitals bought machines more to advertise their sophistication than from any concrete need. These high-cost facilities were seldom used, but still had to be paid for.

That kind of bad judgment does inflate the cost of care, but we suspect that such mistakes do not have so great an impact as critics would have us believe. One forecast of medical expenses estimated that new medical technology alone could add 69 percent to the cost of health care by 2030. However, the Ad Hoc Group for Medical Research Funding, an umbrella organization for some 200 professional societies, patient support groups, and academic associations, points to one credible study of the effects of medical research on health-care costs. Most of the examples involved new drugs or new uses for existing pharmaceuticals, rather than new hardware, but the trend was clear. Each $1 invested in clinical and applied research was repaid by $2 to $3 in annual savings on patient care. In the absence of clearer evidence, this does not seem likely to promote medical inflation.

That leaves the aging of the population. As the giant Baby Boom generation reaches retirement age, beginning in 2011, the number of elderly people in need of medical care will skyrocket. In 1990, there were 31.2 million Americans over age 65, or 12.5 percent of the population. In 2000, the number will be 34.7 million, or 12.6 percent. Thereafter, the retirement-age population rises to 39.4 million in 2010, 53.2 million in 2020, 69.4 million in 2030, and 75.2 million in 2040. By 2040, the over-65 age group will represent more than 20 percent of the population, or nearly triple what it was in 1950.

The "oldest old," those age 85 and older, make up a much smaller fraction of the population, yet one that is important far beyond its size. In the United States, there were just 3 million people age 85 and above as of 1990, or 1.2 percent of the population. By 2010, there will be 5.7 million, or 1.9 percent of the population. In 2030, when the Baby Boomers have begun to reach this stage of life, there will be nearly 8.5 million Americans age 85 or older, or 2.4 percent of the population. And by 2050, the number will reach 18.2 million, or 4.6 percent. The oldest old are the fastest-growing age group in the developed world.

They also are the group with the greatest medical needs. As we have seen, older people spend far more on health care than the young; our average yearly medical bill nearly triples in the twenty years after we reach age 30 or so, and it goes up from there.

In almost all areas of health care, seniors are the primary consumers:

- Most of the $70 billion or so that Americans spend on nursing-home care each year goes for patients over age 65. People of retirement age have a 44 percent chance of spending at least some time in a nursing home. As of 1990, the most recent date for which we have been able to locate data, nearly one person in four aged 85 and over lived in a nursing home.

- In any given year, upward of 1.5 million Americans use home-health-care services. Three-fourths are age 65 and over. Just 3 people out of every 1,000 require home health care between the ages of 45 and 64. Above age 85, the number is 80 people per 1,000 among men and 132 per 1,000 among women.

- Among people aged 65 to 69, only 9 percent require help with personal care, such as eating and bathing. By age 85, that number soars to 45 percent. Many others need assistance with more challenging activities, such as shopping. Some 7.1 million Americans had significant functional problems in 1994, according to Duke University demographers Kenneth Manton, Larry Corder, and Eric Stallard.

- Four out of five patients admitted to hospices are age 65 or older. Fully 13 percent are 85 or above.

- According to Medicare figures, half of all medical spending covered by the program takes place in the last six months of life, fighting an illness that both doctor and patient often know will prove fatal.

The most optimistic estimate we have found suggests that the aging of the American population will raise the cost of health care just 24 percent by 2030. We believe this is significantly low. If the Baby Boomers' health fails as that of previous generations has done, the nation's medical bill could be higher still.

In all, if we carry these trends in population, technology, and inflation forward unchanged, spending on health care could more than triple by 2030, when Baby Boomers finally begin to approach the age of 85. The nation's yearly medical bill then would total somewhere between $3 trillion and $3.5 trillion. Medicare alone would absorb some 7 percent of the GDP in 2030, while the total amount consumed would be nearing 20 percent. Employment in the field would not rise quite so quickly, because simple inflation requires no extra doctors, nurses, or technicians to operate it. But there could easily be 15 million people working in American hospitals and nursing homes, twice as many as there are today. Most of these new jobs would be for nurses, nurse's aides, orderlies, attendants, and others who provide direct patient care.

THE REAL FUTURE

However, all that is the baseline forecast, the one in which science does little or nothing to stem the inroads of time on our health. As we discovered in Chapter 1, it probably has little to do with the future in which we soon will find ourselves. And that returns us to our real question: Given that the health-care industry has evolved largely to serve the needs of the aged, how will life extension change "big medicine"?

We see no prospect at all that health care will grow to anything like the size projected above. This would be true even if life extension never panned out.

Already, there is evidence that even near the end of their lives, current and future generations will be healthier than their parents and grandparents were. One optimistic sign comes from the 1996 Duke University study of disability. The number of significantly disabled people found in that survey, 7.1 million, was actually smaller than most authorities expected. Given the rate of impairment that prevailed in 1982, the projected figure would have been 8.3 million. This reduction, nearly 15 percent of the total once forecast, appears to have occurred because of better habits. Even among today's seniors, diets have improved while smoking and excessive drinking have declined, and we are beginning to see the results.

There is more to come. In a recent book (*Probable Tomorrows: How Science and Technology Will Transform Our Lives in the Next 20 Years,* St. Martin's Press, 1997), we examined some remarkable developments in medicine that seem likely to enter clinical use within the next decade. They included genetic medicine, a possible cure for cancer, and a technique that may allow surgeons to perform organ transplants without fear of rejection by the body. Since then, we have learned of other advances, including two promising discoveries in the treatment of Alzheimer's disease. These new treatments will not dramatically lengthen our lives. Biodemographers S. Jay Olshansky, of the University of Chicago, and Bruce Carnes, of Argonne National Laboratory, have calculated that completely eliminating most major illnesses—heart disease, cancer, and diabetes included—would raise life expectancy to no more than 85 years. Other estimates have put the increase even lower. However, conquering these chronic disorders would dramatically improve our quality of life in later years and sharply reduce our need for care.

Supplements of melatonin and the other hormones that decline with age could push infirmity even farther off, whether or not they actually extend our life span. In Chapter 1, we catalogued some of the benefits that melatonin in particular has conferred in animal and human trials. A second hormone, dehydroepiandrosterone (DHEA), has many beneficial effects in aging animals, while growth hormone has proved to reverse the loss of strength that afflicts elderly human patients. Both melatonin and DHEA bolster the immune system. They improve our ability to resist stress. DHEA appears to reduce the risk of cancer and obesity. There is significant evidence that it may protect against diabetes and heart disease. Drs. Manton and Stallard, the Duke University demographers, working with epidemiologist Burton Singer, of Yale, recently analyzed the data collected by the famed Framingham Heart Study, which followed the health of people in Framingham, Massachusetts, from 1950 through 1984. They calculated that if people had been able to hold their cholesterol levels, blood pressure, and other risk factors to the level of an average 30-year-old, men would have lived to approximately 100 years, women to 97. Melatonin and DHEA could well push our life expectancy to nearly the century mark. All this without even considering the possibility of slowing the aging process itself.

Suddenly, the senior population is beginning to soar. The Social Security Administration estimates that there will be no more than 75.5 million Americans aged 65 and older in the year 2040, when some of the Baby Boom generation are into their 90s. In fact, simply controlling well-known risk factors—many of them amenable to melatonin, DHEA, and conventionally healthy lifestyles—would push the retirement-age population to 127.5 million. Yet very few of them would require the level of health care that seniors routinely need today.

Oddly enough, life extension probably would not enlarge the senior population much more than Manton and his colleagues foresee. Given a life expectancy of roughly a century, most Baby Boomers will still be around forty years from now. The effect of extending life expectancy to 115 or 120 will not be felt until 2050—and that is farther ahead than we really care to speculate.

Where all this leaves health care is hard to quantify. It is clear what kind of changes are coming, but much depends on when life extension is so clearly demonstrated that people begin taking hormone treatments en masse. Until then, health care will continue to absorb more money, and continue as well to provide well-paid employment for more and more people. But sometime, most likely between 2010 and 2015, the trend will reverse itself. People who use anti-aging treatments will begin to grow healthier even as they grow older. And the need for doctors and nurses, hospitals and nursing homes, will begin to decline. So will the number of people employed in this field. In the end, we will have a population of seniors who need little more care than they required in their 30s. If so, the more populous, more prosperous America of 2040 is not likely to spend much more on health care than we do today.

CHAPTER FIVE

OTHER LANDS, SAME PROBLEMS

T hus far, we have considered only the problems that life extension will inflict upon the United States. This suits our own needs, for we are Americans and assume that many of our readers will be as well. Yet this narrow focus is artificial, for even if we ignore the promise of life extension, the trend toward longer life is global and its effects will reverberate throughout the increasingly interlinked world of the twenty-first century.

All of the developed nations confront much the same explosion in their retirement-age populations. After growing slowly for most of this century, their numbers of elderly are poised to skyrocket. Not one of these prosperous lands has prepared to absorb the impact of this change. And they are the ones with the best chance of weathering this change gracefully.

In the past, great age has been limited almost exclusively to the wealthy. In poor countries, life is harsh and almost always brief. However, for the first time even the relatively impoverished lands face a dramatic growth in their numbers of elderly. By definition, they have fewer resources to meet their needs than their more fortunate neighbors do, too few to avoid growing hardship even under a traditional, limited-life scenario. They are still less able to cope with either of the options that life extension brings—the appearance of an enormous cohort of pure consumers or a sudden ballooning of the labor pool. If life in the twenty-first century will be increasingly difficult in the great trading nations, it could be catastrophic in the less developed countries.

Because of these pressures, we can expect a gradual loss of economic and social stability throughout much of the world over the next twenty-five to fifty years. This decline will feed back to aggravate the problems of the United States.

Again, let us begin by examining the "standard model" of global aging. Once we have seen where we are headed today, we can try to figure out how life extension will change the picture.

AN AGING WORLD

Looking around the world, we find that the United States is, in many ways, comparatively well off. Its elderly population is growing, but not to the extent seen in several other lands. And if American leaders sometimes appear deficient in foresight and political will, at least this country has a large and powerful economy to support whatever social efforts it chooses to make on behalf of tomorrow's aged. That strength is not universally found in other countries.

As a group, the member states of the Organization for Economic Cooperation and Development already are beginning to feel the economic and social impact of aging. As of 1990, some 18 percent of their aggregate populations were over 60. By 2030, the number will rise to over 30 percent. People over 80 represent only 3 percent of the population today, but that figure will double over the next few decades. The Baby Boom was not uniquely American.

For a few specific countries, the change will be particularly dramatic. In Britain, which has the oldest population in Europe, one person in five already was over 60 in 1990, the most recent year for which national population statistics allow direct comparison. By 2030, about 28 percent of the population will have reached that age. About 19 percent of French men and women in 1990 were age 60 or older. Over the next three decades, the figure will climb to 29 percent. Japan's over-60 cohort represented about 18 percent of the population in 1990. By 2030, nearly one-third of Japanese will be age 60 or above. One German in five today is age 60 or older. Seniors will make up about 35 percent of the German population in 2030. And in Italy, about 21 percent of the population had already seen its 60th birthday. By 2030, the figure will climb to 36 percent. All of these countries, on average, will be older than the United States.

If Americans already are feeling the pinch of their country's commitment to Social Security and other old-age benefits, other nations are still more heavily burdened. Where the United States now spends about 6.5 percent of its Gross Domestic Product on pensions, the average among OECD members is 9 percent. In France, Germany, Italy, and Japan, pension costs are expected to rise to between 14 percent and 20 percent of the GDP.

Until recently, the luxury of a long life has been limited to the rich countries. In poor lands, where healthy diets and modern medical care are scarce, life expectancy remains at levels the United States, Europe, and Japan have long outgrown. The average man or woman born into the less developed countries in the last five years can expect to live to the age of 62. Their peers in the poorest countries will survive only to 51. In Sierra Leone, very probably the most short-lived nation in the world, life expectancy remains stuck at 39, a figure the United States left behind more than a century ago. Other African nations are not much better off.

Yet as a whole, the developing countries too are aging rapidly. According to demographers at the U.S. Census Bureau, some 56 percent of the world's people age 65 and older live in the poorer lands, and the proportion is growing. Balance off the deaths and the birthdays that occur each day, and the world gains some 800,000 people over age 65 every month. About 70 percent of them live in the developing countries. By 2000, just two years from now, there will be 200 million people over age 60 in the wealthy nations, and 400 million in the developing lands.

In many of these regions, the number of elderly people is comparatively low. Yet the rate of growth remains, with rare exceptions, staggering:

The old are positively rare in Africa and the Middle East, where only 5 percent of the population are over 60. By 2030, seniors still will represent only about 7.5 percent of the population. Over the same period, the number of people over age 75 will grow from about 1 percent of the population to only 1.5 percent. In part, this slow growth represents the impact of AIDS, which in sub-Saharan Africa is rapidly destroying the generation that otherwise would have reached their senior years during the next few decades. It is not seen elsewhere.

In China today, about 9 percent of the population have celebrated their 60th birthday, while about 2 percent are over age 75. By 2030, the country's total population will grow by about 19 percent, thanks to birth-control programs that have reduced fertility from 4.9 births per woman in 1970 to 1.8 today. Yet the elderly population will grow by 72 percent. In 2030, between 22 percent and 25 percent of the Chinese population will be over age 60, depending on the source of the estimate, while more than 6 percent will be over 75.

Even with Japan, Korea, Taiwan, and Singapore to raise the average, the rest of Asia remains well behind China, both in its economic development and in the size of its elderly population. Today, only 7 percent of the region's people are age 60 or older, while perhaps 1 percent are 75 or older. By 2030, there will be just over 8 percent age 60 and above, and more than 3 percent will be age 75 or older.

The traditional socialist countries of Eastern Europe come closest to the developed world in their numbers of elderly. Today, roughly 16 percent of their populations are over 60, about 4 percent over 75. In 2030, the numbers will be 24 percent and 9 percent, respectively. Yet in Russia life expectancy for men is actually dropping at the moment. Continued economic instability in this region could change its outlook significantly.

Finally, consider Latin America and the Caribbean, where poverty and disease are far more common than in neighboring countries to the north. Just 7 percent of the region's population are age 60 or older today, while less than 2 percent are 75 or above. By 2030, nearly 14 percent will be seniors, while about 5 percent will have reached age 75.

OLD MEANS POOR

As simple figures, these numbers do not mean much. But throughout much of the world, the elderly must support themselves, and many find it difficult to do so. Sickness grows far more common as well. As we have already seen, these facts bring with them a heavy social and economic burden, which few nations are well equipped to shoulder.

Let us consider the most fortunate countries first.

European seniors are doing pretty well so far. In Germany as in the United States, older couples actually bring in more than younger ones, about 104 percent of the national median income, on average. Older women on their own are not quite so well off, but their income still remains more than four-fifths of the national median. In France, married couples over age 65 have a median income fully 99 percent that of working-age couples. Even elderly women living alone—the poorest seniors in almost any land—retain about 85 percent of the national median income. For comparison, senior couples in the United States average nearly 110 percent of the national median income, while older women living alone make do with just a bit more than 60 percent of the median.

The reason European seniors make out so well, of course, is that most of the Continent has traditionally enjoyed some of the most lavish pension plans in the world. In a recent survey of seniors in the European Union, more than half of beneficiaries said their pensions were either "completely adequate" or "just about adequate." In Germany, no less than four out of five were satisfied with their pensions.

Such lavish plans cannot be sustained in an aging world. As a fraction of the Gross Domestic Product, pension contributions remain in single digits. Britain contributes barely more than 4 percent of its GDP toward pensions. Italy, Germany, and Japan all contribute about 7 percent of their GDPs, France a bit more than 7 percent. These sums are fixed by law and are not scheduled to change, save in the United States, which actually plans to spend less of its GDP on old-age benefits after 2040.

Yet pension spending will skyrocket. In the United States, retirement benefits will rise to 7 percent of the GDP by 2035 and then will climb slowly to 7.5 percent. In Britain, spending will peak at roughly 5.5 percent around 2035. France will spend about 14 percent of its GDP on pensions by 2035. Japan's pension spending is slated to peak at 16 percent of GDP in 2055. And Germany's old-age benefits will rocket to nearly 18 percent of GDP in just the ten years between 2025 and 2035, gradually declining to 15 percent over the next thirty-five years.

All this means that national debts will rise sharply. Despite the current round of self-adulation from Washington politicians who claim to have balanced the U.S. federal budget, barring dramatic policy changes, America's net debt will grow from about 40 percent of its GDP today to roughly 100 percent in 2030, even as the GDP itself more than doubles. Most of this increase will come from paying the cost of health care for the aged. In Germany and France, where pensions are more generous than in the United States, net debt is expected to double. Japan's net debt today is just 13 percent of its GDP, the smallest among the major developed nations. By 2030, thanks to the rising cost of pension benefits, it will grow to some 300 percent of GDP!

Proportionally, there will be fewer people to pay those benefits. As in the United States, the number of retirees throughout the developed world is growing far more rapidly than the number of working-age people to support them. At present, for each current beneficiary in most countries there are four to five people in their productive years to pay into the national pension plan. By 2030, there will be only three working-age Americans for each pensioner. In most of Europe, there will be only 2.5 potential contributors for each recipient.

Outside these few wealthy nations, prospects are even less promising. The problem is not that pensions will grow beyond affordability, though that often is true. The real trouble is that so few people are covered by them. Only half of the urban workers in China—about 10 percent of the working population—can hope for a pension. In the Chinese countryside, only a few government workers are protected. Indian social security and pension programs cover government employees and a few workers for large corporations. Yet they represent only a tiny fraction of the population. Fully 92 percent of India's people will have nothing to fall back on when they can no longer work. Throughout much of Asia, most of Africa, and parts of Latin America, the situation is even worse. If the world's poor nations can avoid a future of homelessness and starvation for their older citizens, tomorrow's elderly will nonetheless represent an enormous drain on economies that barely support themselves as it is.

OLD ALSO MEANS SICK

Thus far, we have considered only pension benefits. And while some fraction of health-care costs may disappear into the retirement budgets quoted above, medical expenses for the elderly represent one more growing burden that countries will have to carry—or not. Throughout much of the world, health-care spending already is inadequate. The United States spends nearly $2,800 per person on health care, the most of any country in the world. Europe, Japan, and Canada all make do with less, but still provide excellent care. But among countries classified by the World Bank as having a "middle income," such as those of Latin America, annual health spending averages $105 per person. Among poor countries, the average is only $16 per person. The tiniest health budget belongs to Vietnam, just $2 per person.

Most observers believe that the world's health-care systems will be hard pressed to meet the needs even of relatively young people in years to come. Hospitals in the developing lands still are overwhelmed by childhood disorders such as diarrhea and respiratory problems. Lately, changing lifestyles and the first hints of global aging have begun to worsen their burden. Between 1985 and 2000, hospitals in Mexico are seeing admissions for cancer and cardiopulmonary disease rise by some 40 percent. And a recent report from the World Health Organization warns that there is far worse to come. Faced with unfriendly markets at home, America's tobacco companies have been selling hard abroad, with predictable effect. Thanks to a dramatic rise in smoking, the incidence of cancer, heart disease, and pulmonary disorders such as emphysema in Eastern Europe is now the highest the world has ever seen. The 1997 WHO report on global health warns that in the prosperous European Union, lung cancers in women will increase by one-third as soon as 2005. During the same period, European men will suffer a 40 percent rise in prostate cancers. In poorer lands, the study adds, the number of cases of diabetes and cancer will double by 2025.

Even the wealthy nations are finding it difficult to cope with rising medical costs. The poor ones have still less hope. And unless these countries can find some way to bolster their health-care systems, the aging of their populations represents a medical disaster waiting to happen.

SEARCHING FOR SOLUTIONS

Throughout the world, wherever pension and elder-health plans exist, they are being stretched to their limits. Very soon, most countries face a difficult choice. Governments can raise taxes on workers to pay for benefits to the retired—raise them beyond any credible levels. Or they can cut benefits to older people whom they have led to expect a reasonably prosperous retirement. Or, just possibly, they can find some third alternative, which will allow people to live in comfort after they leave the workforce without overburdening those who remain on the job. Several approaches are being tried.

Most developed countries are trying to encourage workers to retire later. They would have to do this even if they could afford to make good on their promises of lavish pensions for all. The Organization for Economic Cooperation and Development recently studied labor prospects for several of the major trading nations. With working-age populations in decline, they found that Germany, Japan, and Italy each will need between 13 million and 15 million workers more than they can expect to have. Unless these countries become considerably more open to immigrants, who eventually will retire themselves, they will have to make up the shortfall from among workers who now expect to stay home and collect their pensions.

Thus many countries increasingly are trying to keep older workers at work, where they continue to pay into retirement funds rather than drawing money out. Like the United States, some countries are raising their retirement ages. However, again like the United States, they are doing it far less rapidly than is needed. In Britain, men now retire at age 65, women at 60. The country is gradually raising women's retirement age to 65 as well, but the process will not be complete until 2020. Germany and Italy have introduced similar incremental plans to delay retirement. Japan's mandatory pension age is now 60, but will climb to 65 early in the next century.

In other countries, however, this necessary process is operating in reverse. In 1982, France reduced its pension age to 60, and "solidarity contracts" introduced over the last decade allow many people to retire at 55. Railway workers end their careers at 55 and meet any attempt at reform with strikes that paralyze the French economy. Sweden had one of the most farsighted retirement plans in the world. With flexible work schedules, part-time jobs, and state subsidies for the labor market, Sweden has kept more older people at work than any of its European neighbors. Unfortunately, growing budget deficits have forced Sweden to cut back, and one of the items cut was the grant program that has encouraged business to retain retirement-age workers in at least part-time jobs. By 2000, the last of the subsidies will be gone. No one knows whether Swedish companies and workers will maintain the habit of phased retirement once that incentive disappears.

They may well not. A recent poll of working-age Europeans found that eight out of ten believed that job recruiters discriminate against older workers. They have evidence to support them. Over the last decade or so, European companies have been downsizing, just as their American competitors have. They have been using much the same technique: encouraging older workers to retire early. Usually, this is accomplished through incentives, but not always. In Japan, employees who fail to take retirement at 55 and make way for the young often are harassed until they accept their banishment.

Though most personnel managers would deny it in public, privately they explain that younger workers are preferred because older ones are more likely to require costly health care, collect whatever pay raises accrue to seniority, and are capable of less physical performance than younger workers. Where technical skills are required, they also are much less likely than younger employees to apply for extra training. Recruiters admit that senior workers usually are more reliable and conscientious than the young, but it seems to make little difference. The reluctance to employ the old—and in this context "old" means anything beyond about age 45—seems universal.

Faced with their own waves of retirees in the next few decades, many countries in Asia and Latin America, which never promised the lavish pension plans once popular in Europe, have been adopting a new style of retirement package. These are mandatory pension and savings programs, which aim to ensure that each worker will lay away enough money during his career to fund his retirement without public aid.

The prototype for these systems was enacted in Chile in 1981. By law, all wage earners there must contribute 10 percent of their earnings (up to a ceiling) to any of several private pension funds. These funds then invest the contributions in stock and money markets. Workers can shift their money from one fund to another at will, an option that keeps fund managers working hard for top returns, but they cannot opt out of the system. When beneficiaries retire, they receive an indexed annuity, based on the amount they contributed. Neither the government nor employers are involved in the process. Unlike the U.S. Social Security program, the Chilean system really does restore to retirees what they put into the system during their working years, plus whatever their investments have earned—and nothing more.

Singapore takes this notion a step further. Not only does this tiny, prosperous land have a compulsory savings plan for workers, it offers tax breaks and preferred access to government housing for people who have elderly relatives living with them.

It is too soon to tell just how well these plans will work. In its first twelve years, Chile's pension funds turned in spectacular results, earning nearly 15 percent per year on average. However, the 1980s and early '90s were boom times for the Chilean economy. There is nothing but the managers' skill to keep these pension funds from losing money in a bear market. We simply do not know yet whether compulsory savings plans will prove a viable way to fund the senior years of an aging world.

The course of health care is clearer, because Europe has pioneered the system other countries will have to adopt. In the United States, medicine is institutionalized. Patients go to their doctors and rely on hospitals and, increasingly, health maintenance organizations for treatment of any but the least troublesome ills. House calls are a thing of the past. In Europe, most care is home care. Though hospitals deal with acute disorders, chronic conditions are handled by visiting doctors and nurses. This cuts costs, is more convenient for elderly patients, and ensures that almost everyone receives quality care. It is a system well suited to lands where resources are limited. We will examine it more closely in Appendix A.

UPSETTING THE APPLECART

This is the future into which medicine is about to drop its most earthshaking breakthrough, a much longer life for all who choose to accept it. We have devoted this much space to the world's current and proposed systems of retirement and health care, not because they have much to offer an age of extended life, but to show that they have so little. Built for short-lived people, already straining at their limits, with no provision at all for the elderly of the poorest lands, they cannot provide for the needs of people who may well plant oak trees as children and then survive to watch them die of old age.

We already have explained our basic reasoning about our prospects of coping gracefully with the transition to longer lives in Chapter 3. Most of what we said about the United States applies equally to the rest of the developed world. No pension system we can imagine will allow tomorrow's workers to retire at 65, and very possibly not at 95. It may not be possible to retire at all, save on personal savings and investments, until we are physically incapable of work. In compensation, it appears that our health will remain sound until far into old age. If we must continue working, at least we should be able to do so. Yet it may be many years before national economies grow to provide employment for all who need it. The early twenty-first century will be a time of difficult transition.

It could be harder still for a reason we have not yet considered at all. To date, the world has limped along despite vast inequities. The United States, Europe, Japan, and a few other countries are enormously wealthy compared with the rest of the world. Asia, Latin America, Africa—continents that are home to nearly 80 percent of the world's population—live largely in abject poverty. Where wealth exists in these regions, it often does so alongside starvation and disease. Once it was possible for the poor to blame their condition on fate, or on the injustice of local rulers. As modern communications systems unite the world into a single community, this view has become nearly impossible to maintain. To many, the riches of distant nations now seem every bit as unjust as those of local landowners. This is one reason that poor, disaffected youth from the Middle East now find solace in committing terrorism against the United States and Europe. Religious and political differences are important, but it would be difficult to recruit suicide bombers among young people with jobs and hope of a better life.

Now picture the response of poor people, without hope, already angry at their condition, who suddenly learn that scientists in the decadent West have discovered the key to something remarkably like eternal youth. Not only do we in the United States, Europe, and Japan live in luxury, now we will continue to do so long after our neighbors elsewhere—and in many cases their *grandchildren!*—have died. It will seem the most monstrous injustice of all.

The transition ahead may be even more difficult than it first appears.

CHAPTER SIX

PLANNING FOR EXTRA DECADES

A sk the 20- and 30-somethings who populate the fabled "Generation X," and you quickly discover that they already know the truth about retirement. Many say that they expect to retire in comfort, probably before age 65. Yet the traditional combination of personal savings and public benefits will not be there for them, and as you probe deeper it becomes clear that they understand. At heart, they know they will never be able to retire. The system that allowed most of the World War II generation, unlike any other in history, a period of rest and relaxation after decades of work is breaking down. It cannot be repaired.

In sharp contrast, almost anyone from the Baby Boom generation still clings to the seductive vision of leisure in the late days of life. Baby Boomers do so despite the overwhelming weight of evidence that generalized retirement was a fluke of history and despite their own failure to prepare for such an endless vacation.

The Boomers' dreams are modeled on the success of the World War II generation, now retired in record numbers. But that success was built on three supports and one spectacular piece of luck. Personal savings, corporate pensions, and Social Security all contributed. Omit any one of them, and today's retirees would have had a much harder time of it. Then the value of their houses shot up at a rate never before sustained over an entire nation for such a long period. Trading down for smaller retirement homes provided the cash, most of it exempt from taxes, to make modest lifestyles luxurious.

None of these special conditions applies to the Boomers. The oldest among them already have turned 50, and on average they have not saved for the future. They do not own investments sufficient to support them in the years after work. Few are covered by corporate pension programs, and fewer still will remain with one company long enough to qualify for whatever benefits might be available. Neither have they benefited from the tremendous run-up in housing values in the '70s and '80s. And no one believes that Social Security will support his or her imagined years of tranquillity and contentment. Yet the great majority of Boomers still expect a traditional retirement. Few even accept that it will begin as late as age 65. Many hope to leave work by age 60, or even 55. The disconnection between their dreams of retirement and the reality of their lives is complete.

Into this misapprehended future comes the prospect of extended life, of retirement periods that if begun at age 65 could stretch on for half a century—longer than our working lives themselves. It just isn't going to happen. The future may not require us to work on, day after increasingly grim day, until we are found slumped over our computer terminals. There are compromises we can make between traditional careers and the World War II generation's comfortable version of retirement, and they may well be more satisfying than the enforced leisure we once expected. Yet it is clear that anyone who is not prepared to retire within the next few years will be forced to adjust his or her plans.

Just how thoroughly aging research will transform our lives and livelihoods depends on when this ultimate medical breakthrough makes itself felt. 2005? 2020? Somewhere in between? For our purposes, it is safest to assume that the change will arrive early, when it will have the greatest impact on us. This provides the incentive to begin planning now, while we still can adjust our goals and expectations to fit our unnaturally long futures.

WHAT WILL YOU NEED?

Statistically speaking, many of our readers will be Baby Boomers, and that means that few of them will have given much effective thought to retirement. Saving for the future, if they are conscious of the need at all, comes last in a long line of budget items. When money gets tight or unexpected bills come due, savings are cut first. This is true even among the oldest Boomers, who now are less than fifteen years from the traditional age of retirement. Under the circumstances, it seems worth asking, what will they need to retire? What will you need?

Financial planners assume that it costs people a bit less to live comfortably during retirement than it did during their working years. By the time we retire, our mortgage should have been paid off, eliminating the single largest drain on our income. Children will have been put through college, which takes care of the other great expense of midlife. Scratch off a couple of lesser costs as well. We no longer have to dress for work, assuming that we did so in the first place, so we will not be paying nearly as much for suits, ties, and dry cleaning. And we will not be commuting to work each day, so our transportation costs decline as well. Eventually, these savings are likely to be offset by rising medical expenses, so our economic position is not quite as good as it first appears. But for daily living expenses, maintaining your accustomed lifestyle will take a retirement income equal to about 80 percent of your peak earnings.

Less of that will come from Social Security than many people realize. Even for those at the bottom of the pay scale, government benefits add up to just 45 percent of working-life income. At $60,000 per year, the maximum FICA-taxed wage in the mid-1990s, they replace a meager 20 percent of income. That leaves somewhere between 35 percent and 60 percent of your former earnings to be made up by private pensions, retirement plans, and other revenue sources. For too many of us, this will come as horrifying news, but there is worse to come. A recent study by Merrill Lynch estimated that as of 1992, Social Security and Medicare combined contributed 19 percent to the average retiree's income. However, it warned that in order to put these programs on a sound financial footing, it will be necessary to halve their benefits no later than 2009. In that case, by 2029, when the youngest Boomers finally reach age 65, the two programs will add only 7 percent to the average beneficiary's income.

Traditional defined-benefit pension plans form an even smaller portion of retirement income. According to the Merrill Lynch study, they provided just 8 percent of the average retiree's nest egg in 1992 and will fall to half that by 2029. The truth, of course, is that for a small minority of today's workers, defined-benefit pensions will contribute a healthy chunk of retirement income. For the great majority, they will supply nothing at all.

Fewer than half of workers now are covered by any pension plan. And of those who are, most come under so-called defined-contribution pensions. This is an important distinction. In the old-style defined-benefit plans, workers knew just how much they were going to receive upon retirement. In defined-contribution schemes, such as the popular 401(k) investment plans, workers contribute a set fraction of their income toward their pension fund. Many companies contribute as well, but nothing in law compels them to do so. How much the beneficiary receives years down the road depends on how well the fund's investments perform. And since many of these plans are controlled by individual workers themselves, rather than by professional money managers, the chance of making a killing with a defined-benefit package looks only a little better than the chance of being killed. Even the most successful investors could find themselves strapped for cash if their portfolios are hit with a bear market just as they are ready to retire.

There are other problems as well. Most companies demand that new hires stay with the firm for a year before they can join the pension plan. Workers can bring their existing 401(k) plans with them, but it will be twelve months before contributions begin again. Every time you change jobs—four or five times per career in today's employment market, and the number is growing—you lose a year's worth of savings.

Many lose far more, even while they are covered. Only 70 percent of the workers eligible for defined-contribution pensions take advantage of them, and most save far less than they should. Legally, workers may contribute up to 25 percent of their income to a 401(k) plan, up to a generous maximum, which changes periodically. Despite this, the average worker who participates in a defined-contribution plan socks away less than $2,000 per year. Of course, the other 30 percent save nothing at all, and they miss out on their employers' contributions as well.

To ensure a comfortable retirement, Merrill Lynch estimated, the average two-career family between 35 and 45 years old need to save 19 percent of their after-tax income, if they are among the lucky few who are covered by defined-benefit pensions. Others should be saving fully one-fourth of their income, either in a defined-contribution plan or as private investments. And that does not include any savings to pay their children's way through college. Instead, the average couple set aside just 7 percent of their after-tax income. An estimated 20 million people have no savings at all.

Add it all up, and most of today's workers will find that they cannot afford to retire in comfort. Many will not be able to retire at all. As of 1992, some 27 percent of the average senior's income arrived as wages for a post-"retirement" job. By 2029, current earnings will account for 41 percent of the average retiree's income. Anyone who has only Social Security and Medicare to fall back on will have to earn fully 93 percent of his or her desired income. So much for retirement!

The picture may be even worse than it appears, because retirement planners assume that seniors will tap their savings in order to supplement their investment profits. This reduces their income, so maintaining their lifestyle means spending a bit more of their principal each year. Inflation too will gradually erode their wealth. Even without unexpected medical bills and other extraordinary expenses, by the age of 80 or so the average retirees' money will be gone. Of course, according to the actuarial tables, so will they. It all works out.

Now how much must we save during our working years to support a retirement that could last until we are 115 or 120 years old? The obvious answer is, more than anyone can if they depend on a salary for their living. Especially those aging Baby Boomers who, already pushing 50, have hardly begun to salt money away. This will be true even if the technology that extends our lives also protects us from the hospital bills that plague today's seniors. Even at the rate of 1 or 2 percent per year, if inflation has half a century in which to act, it will eat away the buying power of our savings and investments while we still have need of them.

What will you need to retire? It was a trick question. In an age of healthy, energetic centenarians, traditional retirement will be possible only for the independently wealthy. Most Boomers, like their younger colleagues, will remain on the job long beyond the time when nature would have had them dead. In the past, we hoped for ten or fifteen years of comfortable retirement. That dream remains realistic. But in the twenty-first century, it will mean that superannuated Baby Boomers finally retire, not at age 65, but around their hundredth birthday!

That may not be all bad, of course. Over a life as long as tomorrow's seniors can expect, the traditional retirement of golf and hobbies could wear a bit thin.

THE NEW WORLD OF WORK

Unfortunately, if retirement is not what it used to be, neither is working life. And the ways in which it has changed will make it difficult to pursue a career that must span three or four extra decades.

At the moment, the country is prosperous. The American economy has created more than 11 million new jobs since 1993. Productivity is rising, even in the once-stagnant service industries. Unemployment is at its lowest level since 1973. Many companies, unable to hire enough skilled people and belatedly recognizing the benefits of institutional memory, have even begun to take back a few of those graying 50-plus executives they once forced out. According to a *Time*/CNN poll in May 1997, only 19 percent of Americans fear for their jobs, down from 30 percent as recently as 1996. Yet all that could change, and it probably will, more than once, before the Boomers retire.

Over the last decade or so, even the most complacent among us have gotten the message. The era of lifetime employment was just wishful thinking for most workers. Today it's history. No job is really secure in the modern global economy. No pension is safe. No plan for the future will survive without frequent revision. The twenty-first century will be even more fluid, more demanding, than the late twentieth.

Security no longer means a corporate guarantee that your job will be there as long as you need it. Technology replaces people with computers, wipes out established markets, and creates dozens of new ones. Global competition opens export jobs for skilled workers, but it destroys opportunities for well-paid drones whose tasks can be performed offshore by assemblers and technicians who earn only a fraction of their salary and benefits. The management pyramid is now a management pancake, and promotions are hard to come by because there is nowhere to be promoted *to*. The old command-and-control hierarchy by which companies used to run their operations has been replaced by project-oriented teams of specialists, who may or may not still have a job when the assignment is over. In this context—call it the real world, as opposed to the sheltered workplace culture that grew up in the 1950s—the only security is your store of transferable skills and experience, the assets that will enable you to find a new job when you need it. Aside from a salary, about all any company can offer is the opportunity to build your own competence, so that your next employer will find you even more valuable than your last, for so long as that employer's changing needs coincide with your growing abilities.

In this challenging environment, tomorrow's artificially youthful seniors will have both advantages and handicaps in competing for a livelihood.

As a group, their chief asset may be simply that life extension will come first to the Boomers, and there are so many of them. In today's job market, a 50-year-old executive who gets laid off has a tough time finding a job, and a 60-year-old is virtually unemployable except as a CEO or a store clerk. Forty years from now, 80-year-old Boomers looking for work will find as often as not that 90-year-old Boomers are doing the hiring. Those overage personnel managers will be very happy to see applicants who can remember when the Beatles broke up.

To the extent that experience translates into wisdom, those ancients will be well placed to head the project teams of tomorrow's companies. Managing others is a skill that only gets better with practice; no one in 2038 will have had more practice than someone who first went job-hunting in 1970. And anyone who can think back far enough to say "Been there; done that; it didn't work" will save his or her employers a lot of wasted time and money.

For any but the most diligent, however, the same decades that give them experience could prove to be their biggest obstacle to survival. As technology permeates our lives, it is becoming ever more important to keep skills up to date. It also is becoming ever more difficult. As mentioned before, the half-life of an engineer's professional knowledge today is only five years. Earn your master's in digital electronics at age 25, and half of what you learned is obsolete by the time you are 30. And progress is accelerating on all fronts. By 2050, when the oldest Boomers are finally ready to begin their fifteen years of retirement, everything humanity knows today will represent just 1 percent of the knowledge then available. For the life-extended, the constant pressure to update old skills, decade after decade without end, will be a heavy burden. It will be all too easy to fall behind.

And simply keeping your core skills up to date will not be enough. What companies want today, and will need even more urgently in the years to come, is a varied background, with just the optimum mix of experience for the task at hand. The leader of a product-development team cannot get by with being a top engineer. Experience in manufacturing, marketing, finance, and a host of other specialties also is required. Already, employees at major corporations are forced to guess what skills their companies will need a year or two further on and take the appropriate courses on their own time. Then, if they picked the wrong specialties, they get to go looking for work elsewhere, their old job gone to someone who guessed right. Twenty years of loyal service with the same firm—an increasingly rare accomplishment—will not protect them from this competitive pressure. And in future the penalty for failure will be a quick plunge from career status to unskilled labor.

At the societal level, even success will bring problems, for each life-extended worker who continues his or her career will displace a younger job seeker whose future looks increasingly bleak. Already, the millions of Boomers in the employment market, combined with the flattening of corporate structures, are making it difficult for their juniors to earn a living. Twenty- and 30-something Generation Xers today earn between 35 percent and 40 percent less in real terms than the Boomers did at the same stage in their careers. By 2020,

with most of the Vietnam cohort still at work and another generation or two of young people competing for places in the economy,
unemployment could reach crisis levels. In the end, government
may be forced to enact incentives and penalties designed to speed
long-lived workers into retirement, whether they want to go or not.

BRACING FOR CHANGE

The key to survival for life-extended Boomers will be a kind of flexibility the World War II generation never needed. Long-term goals
are mandatory, but long-term plans are out. The best job for you is
not the one with the highest salary or richest benefits, but the one
that offers the best chance to broaden your skills. It may be within
the same company, in which case you will have to apply for it just
like any outsider. It may be with the competition, or in a different industry altogether. Or it may be whatever make-do job will keep you
afloat while you take graduate-level courses or professional training.
No option can be overlooked. No plan can go unrevised whenever
an opportunity beckons or a new idea dawns.

- **For a start, give up the notion of a traditional retirement at
  or before age 65.**

  Unless your economic position is rock-solid, you could eventually be forced back to work. And it turns out that the penalty for a
few years of retirement is much too severe. Economist Charles
Brown, of the University of Michigan, once surveyed a group of
men who had taken early retirement and then returned to work.
Most were skilled white-collar workers, and none were older than 63
when they went job-hunting. Yet they had been forced to accept pay
cuts that averaged 40 percent of their previous salaries. Better to remain on the job, if possible, until you are absolutely certain that
you will never have to return.

  There are alternatives, however. You may decide to start your
own business; "retire" to a farm like the one you grew up on and
work sixty hours a week for yourself instead of forty or so for some-

one else; become a teacher and pass your hard-won skills on to a new generation; or even join the Peace Corps, as a surprising number of retirees have done. Or you may find, just before you qualify for one of those rare pensions, that your longtime employer no longer needs you and you have no choice but to scramble for a living at an age when you hoped leisure would be at hand. What you are not likely to do is play golf and putter around the house.

- **If you are not already saving for the future, it is long past time to begin.**

If you are, then try to save more. Financial planners advise that everyone should have savings equal to a year's living expenses before he or she even begins to worry about a retirement fund. Even in today's tight job market, it can take that long for a displaced executive to find another position. Sickness, legal problems, or other unforeseen costs can easily drain the equivalent of a year's salary.

Now let's set a reasonable savings target. Assume that you will manage to invest your "retirement" nest egg wisely enough so that you can eventually siphon off 10 percent per year for living expenses without touching the principal. (Few achieve even that level of profit, year in and year out, good times and bad.) In that case, you need to save ten times as much in investment capital as you hope to spend each year. If your family income is $60,000—a fairly modest sum these days—and you want a post-career income equal to 80 percent of that, you will need to save up $480,000 to meet your goal. Bank fully 25 percent of your current income, and it still will take you thirty-two years to build your retirement fund! With a bit of luck, investment profits could speed the process, but figure on at least twenty years of scrimping before you can begin to collect your reward. Even that is unlikely to support the kind of retirement that you probably hoped for—you will have to pay your own way for many years longer than previous generations did—but at least it is a start.

Here are some other suggestions. No one of them will offer a complete solution for your circumstances and goals. Yet most of these prescriptions apply to everyone. Some combination of them should see you through.

- **Keep learning.**

It does not matter how secure your current job or business appears to be. As the twenty-first century ticks away, the number of people seeking a living will grow much faster than the national economy. Competition for every niche will tighten for the next forty years, as the Baby Boomers vie with their children and grandchildren for a place in the job market. The only way to survive is to remain on the cutting edge in your core specialty and to build ancillary skills to supplement it. It is not enough to be a competent accountant; you also need experience in marketing, manufacturing, team management, and many similar fields. The most successful salesman will have to master the other skills of running a business. Even artists and writers, whose unique personal vision differentiates them from their competition, will have to be proficient at public speaking, the use of graphics and layout software, and Web-page design, just for a start. In any field, constant training is the only way to compete.

Learning is even more important for those who lack a well-paid career and work instead in the blue-collar fields. The most recent employment projections from the Bureau of Labor Statistics extend only to 2005, but they show trends that will continue for many years to come. Manufacturing jobs have vanished by the million over the last twenty years; another 12 percent of the remainder will have disappeared in the decade ending in 2005. Professional specialty jobs are the fastest-growing group, and also will add the most new jobs during the period, some 5 million in all. Job growth will be over 14 percent in all categories that require an associate's degree or better, but less than 14 percent in any category open to someone with only a high school diploma. Jobs that demand a master's degree or doctorate will grow by 29 percent. Fields requiring a year or less of on-the-job training will grow by only 5 percent, the slowest of any category.

At the same time, American schools, on average, have not been doing their job. Though educational performance is finally improving, dropout rates remain at about 25 percent overall, and only half of high school graduates go on to college. Thus three-fourths of the people entering the job market in the coming years will be looking for work in the slowest-growing fields.

In short, the competition for tomorrow's jobs will be greatest exactly where opportunities are hardest to find. A poor general education and the lack of marketable job skills will guarantee a life of poverty and frustration. The only way for today's blue-collar workers to find even minimal security is to train for a new career in the white-collar world. Tomorrow morning would not be too soon to begin.

- **Cultivate multiple revenue sources.**

Even when you have a solid career, secondary income can come in handy. One software designer we know is a part-time woodworker. For him, the tactile experience of wielding century-old hand tools on rich wood surfaces provides a welcome break from the abstractions of his high-pressure workplace. The hobby also produces classic New England furniture that sells well to tourists in the shops of his New Hampshire hometown. His wife, a medical secretary, also writes for the local newspaper. If either of them loses his or her job, this secondary income will cushion the blow. Until then, the profits—nearly $10,000 in an average year—are divided between their daughter's college fund and their investment portfolio. Neither of them is covered by a pension plan, and neither intends to retire. But twenty years from now, they expect to leave their primary occupations and pursue woodworking and writing full-time. Unlike full retirement, it is a goal they should have no trouble accomplishing.

- **Consider self-employment.**

For many executives displaced late in their careers, building their own business has proved the only way to keep going. However difficult the transition, they have discovered the advantages of taking their livelihood into their own hands. Chief among them: The only boss who can never fire you without warning looks back at you from the mirror.

An acquaintance of ours spent almost thirty years testing small computers, working in the same laboratory while his division passed repeatedly from one corporate owner to another. Eventually, the latest owner closed the test lab, and he and his colleagues found themselves on the street. He took early retirement with a modest pension and now consults part-time for his former coworkers, who bought their last employer's equipment and set up their own testing service. He and his wife also purchased a coffee-and-bagel shop in their hometown. He gets up at 4:00 A.M. each day to pick up fresh bagels from a specialty baker. She abandoned a long string of dead-end secretarial jobs to run the operation. Of self-employment, he comments ironically: "We have more money now than we ever did, but neither of us has time to spend it." Being unable to retire does not disappoint him, however. He was raised on a Maine potato farm, where his 90-year-old father still puts in a full day's work. To him, the idea of complete leisure never seemed entirely real. As it turns out, he was right.

- **Plan to retire in stages, and perhaps earlier than we have advised.**

Although retirement at 65 seems a lost cause, you eventually may have little choice but to end your career. As the working population explodes and unemployment figures begin to mount, Americans will call on their government to solve the problem. At first, Washington is likely to offer training programs in an attempt to give the jobless career skills that can earn them a living. In the end, it will turn out that there simply are not enough openings for all who need them. At that point, all those held-over Boomers will come under fire. Congress may enact high taxes on the incomes of seniors who work more than, say, twenty hours per week. It might offer incentives for those who leave a full-time career for semiretirement. Just conceivably, it could find more subtle ways to accomplish its goal. The effect will be to make it easier to leave work, even with a significant loss of income, than to remain on the job. If Boomers still dominate the business world, legislation will be the only way to provide opportunities for their juniors.

The way to avoid this, and to have a pleasanter life in the process, is to cut back voluntarily. Whenever you can afford it, forget work weeks that stretch beyond forty hours, and work part-time. Flexible working schedules are becoming commonplace these days. Well before 2010, most companies will offer job sharing, permitting one part-time employee to split duties with another. (Smart companies will team seniors with younger employees, for whom they can act as mentors.) Anyone so inclined can use the new hours of freedom to develop a hobby into a small business. Otherwise, partial retirement will prove a valuable transition, inoculating habitual workers against the shock of retiring only to find that they have nothing to do.

- **Consider alternative living arrangements.**

Almost everyone prefers to remain in his or her own home so long as health permits. In someone else's house, privacy is little more than a memory, and even one's own much-loved children grow tiresome after a while. Yet at both ends of the age spectrum, people are living in multigenerational and group homes at a rate not seen in decades. The reason is money. With real earnings far below those once available to their parents, many workers in their 20s and 30s cannot afford to buy a house or rent an apartment on their own. So they move back in with their parents or band together in shared housing. Many seniors are strapped for cash, despite Social Security, Medicare, and often a pension. So they move in with their offspring. Three-generation households are so common that there even is a magazine dedicated to Boomers struggling to cope with having their parents and children underfoot.

Many life-extended Boomers will find themselves in the same position. Bereft of pensions, with scant government benefits and too little invested, they will find that life is better when they live it in comfortable surroundings, even if that means sharing with relatives or strangers. For some Boomers, this will be just a return to their youth, when communes and "crash pads" were commonplace. Others will find that the idea takes some getting used to. But simple arithmetic will convince many of tomorrow's long-lived seniors that housing shared is housing they can afford. This is one more option to bear in mind.

We will be the first generation to enjoy the benefits of aging research. Because this change is so novel and so unexpected, preparing for extended life will be one of the greatest challenges we ever face. Future generations will know how long a life to plan. They will have developed mechanisms for allocating society's resources among those who need them. But we can only take it on faith that science will deliver what it now so clearly promises. By the time we know for certain that our own lives will be longer than nature intended, many of us will have entered our traditional retirement years, when our preparations for an extended life should be well under way. Society will not yet have adjusted itself to ease our transition.

Given the alternative, most people are likely to feel that extra decades of healthy, vital life are well worth the trouble it will take to make them comfortable and secure. But reshaping our personal futures will be difficult, and the penalty for being unprepared will be long years of poverty and stagnation. Already, it is time to begin.

CHAPTER SEVEN

ENDURING VALUES FOR EXTENDED LIFE

W henever science frees us from aging, it will precipitate a crisis of values. This is almost by definition. Whenever history brings a dramatic change in the terms of human existence, we scramble to reinterpret our relationships with life and death, with other people, and with the Divine. In this case, the transition is likely to be particularly difficult, because the alteration will strike at the most basic aspect of life, that we all will grow old and die. When that immemorial fact no longer holds true, all else will become open to question.

We have seen such times of liberation before. They tend to be periods of exuberance and chaos, followed by a prolonged societal hangover. In the United States, we have been trying to regain our spiritual balance ever since World War I swept away the political and economic order of the nineteenth century, and with them values that most people had come to take for granted. Driven by war, economic stress, and the rise of technology, successive waves of hedonistic experiment and repressive conservatism have swept the land throughout this century. The Baby Boom generation has first rejected and then reaffirmed the bedrock values of an earlier time. Our cities are plagued by feral children who have neither learned traditional values nor found new ones to guide their lives. The nation's penal systems are swollen beyond capacity with prisoners jailed for trading in drugs that the Boomers who now condemn them once experimented with themselves. Political consensus eludes us, and even practical compromise grows increasingly difficult to achieve.

Such perversities are typical of transition periods. Once the first wave of enthusiasm has crested, reaction sets in. For a time, societies alternately experiment with new standards and retreat to the values they once knew. Eventually, some new consensus emerges, usually from a generation that never knew a world in which the old standards were unchallenged.

This time, the transition is likely to be especially prolonged, as the older generation remains with us. We will not attempt to forecast whatever new consensus eventually will rise out of the chaos to come. At best, we can identify some of the important issues soon to be debated.

LONGER LIFE

The prospect of life extension itself does not seem to be one of them. Ronald A. Carson heads the Institute for Medical Ethics at the University of Texas Medical Branch at Galveston, the only formal ethics program at a U.S. medical school. "We're all going to die of something," he commented. "The longer we can stay healthy up to the time of our demise, more power to us. I cannot think of a reason not to undertake that kind of research.

"It does solve one of our major problems," he added. "As things stand, we spend a lot of money keeping people alive in the last year of their lives. If life extension will obviate that necessity, we are clearly ahead."

Unexpectedly, theologians we contacted in preparing this discussion viewed the prospect of life extension just as calmly as the secular ethicists did. The end of aging seemed to them just one more in a very long line of medical advances.

"I see nothing wrong with extending life, or extending good health in the course of a life," commented Monsignor Robert Paul Mohan, professor emeritus of philosophy at the Catholic University of America, in Washington, D.C., and a specialist in medical bioethics. "I would like to see details of how it will be accomplished, but in principle it sounds fine."

Sister Carol Taylor, an ethicist at Holy Family College, in Philadelphia, who specializes in the problems of aging, observed that "in the Catholic Church, we have a vocation to relate to God. If something gives us more time to do that, I guess it would be good." She did note, however, that "the Church says that the full perfection of life isn't here, so extending life is not an absolute value. There is a time at which we're called home."

"I see no problem with increasing longevity," said Rabbi Arnold Fink, of Beth El Hebrew Congregation, in Alexandria, Virginia. "In the Jewish faith, a long life is considered desirable. In scripture, one of the rewards for good work is that you will live a good long life. This is specifically a reward for honoring your parents. Moses lived to the age of one hundred twenty. One of the things traditionally wished to a Jewish person on his birthday is 'May you live to one hundred twenty.'

"Judaism has always placed a great premium on medicine and physicians," he added. "Many of our great thinkers and philosophers have been physicians, like Maimonides. The Christian community has splinter groups such as the Christian Scientists and the Jehovah's Witnesses, who reject blood transfusions and other medical procedures that might prolong their lives. Nothing of that sort exists among Jews."

Most of the problems that concerned ethicists, secular and religious alike, dealt with the practical side of life extension. "Who benefits?" asked Sister Carol Taylor. "Will this be affordable, or available only to the elite? Will it create an underclass of people who die naturally, either by choice or because they cannot afford treatment? If I decide to opt for a natural life, will I be considered a wimp for not hanging on as long as possible?"

Medical ethicist Ronald Carson observed, "We already face real problems of sharing resources across the generations. We are only slowly learning how to do that. This is really a set of economic and social problems with a moral component. Already, there is an ageist backlash afoot with regard to continued funding of Medicare and Social Security. The social problems created by the prospect of living until well beyond the hundred-year mark are difficult even to imagine at this point."

That question of sharing goes far beyond generational concerns, he believes. "This just raises the question of justice and equity to a higher level," Carson said. "Would this be limited to people in the rich countries? Strictly from a practical viewpoint, it seems that it would be in our best interest to help the poor develop to become our collaborators and to provide markets for our goods, rather than to let them watch enviously, living in poverty and dying young as we live on and on in comparative luxury. But there is a strong moral component to these concerns. Given our history and the values we espouse, it will be very difficult to watch this division of life between the few and the many, with the few largely in the developed world. I don't see how we can just stand by and let it happen. How could we think of ourselves as a land of opportunity if the opportunity for a longer, healthier life were foreclosed by economic or demographic factors?"

One more concern stood out as well; for each of the ethical and religious thinkers we consulted, it was the most important of all. This was the question of meaning.

"What are people going to be doing with their extra time?" asked Courtney Campbell, a specialist in bioethics and religious studies at the University of Oregon, in Corvallis. "It is one thing to give them extra time. It is quite another thing to give them the quality of life they want. This is a social and economic question. We already have enough trouble trying to provide meaning in the life of the elderly in their post-retirement years. If it drags on for an extra three or four decades, I don't know how people will cope with it."

"The questions of quality of life and meaning of life are the crucial ones," agreed Galveston's Ronald Carson. "To live a long, meaningless life seems absurd."

According to Rabbi Fink, "Already, a major issue in the Jewish community is, how do we create meaningful existence for people? Given active minds and healthy bodies, given a lengthy time beyond what we consider to be the present life span, this can only become more important. It is up to the religious community to see how people can make productive lives. The meaning of life becomes essential, rather than the fact of life. It must be redefined at various phases."

This was a major concern for Sister Carol Taylor as well. "We would have to convert society to provide meaningful lives for people living to one hundred fifteen," she said. "If I retire at seventy and have forty years ahead of me, what are those forty years going to look like? It is not enough even to be healthy, if all it means is going out to play golf every day. We will need a major transformation in society to provide a meaningful life for all these people.

"One thing that interests me is our ability to be with others in ways that are not work-oriented," she continued. "If we have to care for someone, a sick child or parent, even if we love them, we tend to resent it because it takes us away from the things we think we should be doing, and that almost always means work. If friend calls and asks whether I would like to go bike-riding on Saturday, I say, 'Gee, I'd love to, but I don't have time.' This may be characteristically American; I don't really know. But we are going to have to find ways to be together in a community and value that in itself, rather than simply because it contributes to work. This is something we need right now. Making our lives substantially longer will just add to this need."

ENDLESS LIFE

If the notion of living longer presented few problems, the next step was another matter. What happens if it turns out that life can be extended indefinitely?

"I can recast the Biblical statement that the days of our lives are threescore and ten to read fourscore, or even one hundred fifty, years," Arnold Fink mused. "But once you cross the line between prolonging life and creating a vision of eternal life, you've made not just a quantitative but a qualitative leap. Human vision has always been measured by our awareness of our own mortality. It does not make any fundamental difference how long we live. The question is still there. If we might theoretically live forever, the implications are staggering.

"Imagine a world in which those who are born could live forever. We would have to rethink birth. Who would determine who would populate this world? Who would determine which families would have the right to have children?

"Going back to Malthusian principles, I would imagine that this might lead to a very violent world. We could see the celebration of violence as curtailing overpopulation. This is very frightening stuff.

"Suicide then becomes a major threat also—people who just decide they've had enough. What happens to our societal position that suicide is something that we simply are not prepared to accept?

"This would cause major, major consternation in the religious community," Rabbi Fink concluded. "We would have to reconsider our whole existence. I'm going to have to think about this for a long time."

Sister Carol Taylor was equally nonplussed. Though not theoretically opposed to life extension, she had already rejected the notion for herself. "If you were to guarantee me an extra forty years, of good quality, I would not take it," she declared. "I think I am doing important work, but other people will be able to carry it on after I'm gone. When I am called home, I will be ready to go. It would be different if I thought that this life is all there is. But when you have faith, asking whether I would want to live longer is like asking a fetus whether it would rather spend an extra four months in the womb. Of course not. There is something better after this."

Given that perspective, the concept that life might be extended indefinitely seemed to come as a shock. "I don't know that it would threaten religious faith," she said, "because it does not change my sense that there is a God. However, it would force us to redefine our idea of creaturehood, of being one of God's creatures. I feel that it's our purpose to grow and develop as human beings. Does this mean that it is now part of being human to live and develop forever?

"This brings us back to the question we considered a few minutes ago. If you believe there is more to existence than the here and now, then living forever is not necessarily good. Barring fatal injury, moving on would be matter of our choosing. We would have to understand when we were being called home. Right now, death is one thing we don't have full dominion over. This would give us full dominion over it.

"This would be the ultimate challenge to many of the Church's teachings," she concluded. "I just don't know how to respond."

SHARED VALUES

What core values must we uphold if mankind is to survive and prosper in an increasingly complex and fragile world? Author Rushworth M. Kidder, founder of the Institute for Global Ethics, in Camden, Maine, asked himself that question several years ago. At the time, he was thinking about such issues as crime, ecocatastrophe, and the often bloody clashes between religious doctrines. However, it seems a valid concern for a world on the verge of a change so fundamental as life extension.

To answer it, Kidder toured the world, talking with two dozen philosophical and religious thinkers, educators, writers, and leaders in business and politics. Among them were Reuben Snake, a Native American leader who died in 1993; Shojun Bando, a prominent Japanese Buddhist monk; Father Bernard Przewozny, a Franciscan and an environmentalist; and Jeane Kirkpatrick, a conservative Republican luminary and former U.S. ambassador to the United Nations. Once his interviews were complete, he tried to distill from their comments a few key values that they all seemed to share. He identified eight, a global code of values for humanity. "Not *the* code," he emphasized, "but *a* code." Those universal values were:

- **Love.** "The base of moral behavior is first of all solidarity, love, and mutual assistance," said Graca Machel, the former first lady of Mozambique. Others spoke of a spontaneous outpouring of compassion and support and the assumption that on the personal level people would help one another. It was love of a very practical form that concerned Kidder's advisers.
- **Truthfulness.** "You should not obtain your ends through lying and deceitful practices," declared former Harvard president Derek Bok in a view that many echoed.
- **Fairness.** "I relate fairness to treating other people as I would want to be treated," commented James A. Joseph, an African American minister who serves as president of the Council of Foundations, in Washington, D.C. Others viewed the concept as being closely related to equality, regardless of race or sex. In fu-

ture, we will add age to the list of barriers across which people are equal and must be treated fairly.

- **Freedom.** Everyone shares the right to believe, speak, and act without undue restraint by government, military conquerors, or other authorities. "Without the principle of individual conscience," said Oscar Arias, a Nobel laureate and former president of Costa Rica, "every attempt to institutionalize ethics must collapse."

- **Unity.** Balanced against individual needs and values was the demand for attention to the collective good. Carried to the extreme, Father Bernard Przewozny, a prominent Catholic theologian, believed, individualism is "destructive of social life, destructive of communal sharing, destructive of participation." Said Dame Whina Cooper, founder of the Maori Women's Welfare League, in New Zealand, "God wants us to be one people."

- **Tolerance.** "The more you say 'Values are important,' " observed John W. Gardner, founder of the citizens' lobby Common Cause, among many other distinctions, "the more you have to say, "There are limits to which you can impose your values on me.' " Others saw in this the broader value of respect for diversity. "In some sense," commented environmentalist Kenneth Boulding, "I feel about the Catholic Church the way I feel about the blue whale: I don't think I'll be one, but I would feel diminished if it became extinct."

- **Responsibility.** Hand in hand with concern for individual rights came the demand for individual responsibility. "This is Confucius's teaching," said Nien Cheng, who grew up in Confucian schools in Peking and eventually converted to Christianity. "You must take care of yourself. To rely on others is a great shame." "We are responsible for our grandchildren," added A. H. Halsey, professor of social and administrative studies at Oxford University and a fellow of Nuffield College. "We will make [it] easier or more difficult for our grandchildren to be good people by what we do right here and now."

- **Respect for life.** This was the paramount value, the only one to be explicitly stated by more than half of Kidder's thinkers. "I was prime minister [of Lebanon] for seven and one-half years," summarized Salim El Hoss. "I can't imagine myself signing a death penalty for anybody in the world. I think that is completely illegitimate, and I [think] that is the kind of thing a code of ethics should deal with."

Other values and other issues arose in Kidder's interviews— peace, stability, the courage to act on one's beliefs, concern for racial harmony, women's roles, and the environment. But these eight were basic, both the least common denominator of universal ethics and of the highest worth, the values that seemed so self-evident that they needed no other justification.

It will not be easy to build on this foundation an ethical structure capable of guiding us through the transition to longer, perhaps unlimited, life. Neither will it be easy to find among these universal truths the individual sense of meaning that can support our own extended lives. Yet this necessity will face us all during the disorienting transition to our own unexpectedly long futures. By distilling the world's wisdom into these eight enduring values, Kidder has offered us one good place to begin the process.

FIVE CHALLENGES FOR THE PERIMORTAL WORLD

In a profile of Steven Spielberg, *Time* magazine writers Richard Corliss and Jeffrey Ressner mused on the nature of aging. "Now he is 50," they said of the Hollywood director, "and 50 is an age for realists. A man takes stock of his dwindling physical inventory and starts thinking not of empire building but of simple maintenance in health, family, and career—the preservation, for just a few more years, dear God, of the suddenly precious status quo. Growth is measured in the spreading acreage around the waist, or in that weird cyst on your neck that makes you wonder if you've been infiltrated by aliens. The people you work with, who used to be older and as stuffy as your parents, are now younger, as mysterious as your kids, and taking over. Fifty is a time for holding on, for hoping that time and gravity will not pull you down . . . quite yet." So it has been, at whatever age our middle years have begun, for as long as humanity has had leisure for reflection.

Now that is about to change, and many other things as well. Ten or twenty years into the future, a time that most of the Vietnam generation and many of their elders will live to see, 50 will be just another birthday, less than halfway along life's path. It will be clear that science has the power to extend our lives and health, not just to the 110 or 120 years it then will have achieved, but on into the indefinite future. Our fears of aging will be obsolete. So will most of the economic and social structures we have built to support our lives and societies. The tensions and pressures of this transition will strain conventions and resources at every turn, many of them not obviously related to the former brevity of our life span.

This change will come upon us with breathtaking speed. Two decades after life-extending therapies enter general use, the developed lands will bulge with youthful octogenarians, and probably some centenarians who were both foresighted and lucky at the critical moment. We will have little opportunity for adjustment to our new circumstances. It will be difficult enough to revise our own individual plans to fit so unexpectedly long a life. For nations and for the world at large, the problems will be incomparably more complex and hard to solve. At this level, making a smooth transition to a future without aging will be all but impossible.

The troubles soon to face us are legion, and to single any of them out as important or pressing is to imply that others can safely be neglected. They cannot. Yet some of the more predictable challenges are of such generality and scope that they deserve special mention. We must consider how to meet them during this "perimortal" time, the few years of uncertainty during which humanity will pass from the mortal to the postmortal era.

It seems that no society ever really meets a challenge before it becomes a crisis. No doubt this transition will be no different. Yet whatever thought we give these issues now should ease our labors when the time for action finally arrives.

We have five candidates for immediate consideration. It turns out, no doubt predictably, that most would require our attention even if aging research were not about to rewrite all of society's rules.

A DECENT LIVING FOR ALL

How does a society give its people an adequate income when tens of millions are unemployed through no fault of their own? It is a question we are almost sure to face during the extended working lives of today's adults.

In Chapter 6, we considered what individuals could do to prepare for a longer life. All we had to offer was commonsense suggestions that would benefit almost anyone, even during a brief natural existence. Save and invest as much as possible. Seize every chance to learn new skills and update existing ones. Develop alternative sources of income against the day when today's career comes to its end. Only the scale and urgency of our needs will change as our lives grow longer.

Advice of this kind rarely does much good, and we doubt that ours will prove more successful than any other. For many people, the prospect of a longer life will not seem real enough to justify changing their habits until it is much too late. Others, however motivated, will find that they cannot adapt to a global marketplace that grows more competitive and more dependent on technology with each passing day. And tomorrow's economy will severely test even the best-equipped job hunters.

For most applicants, few jobs will be available. Most of the occupations that once gave high school graduates a living wage are now obsolete, thanks to modern technology. The remainder are disappearing quickly. The jobs that have replaced them—for computer engineers, biotechnologists, medical technicians, and other such specialists—require training and experience that few of us can acquire at midlife. This imbalance between skills needed and skills available can only grow, despite our best efforts to retrain ourselves for new occupations. In the years to come, Baby Boomers who remain in the employment market will be joined by whole new generations of job seekers. The number of potential workers will grow far beyond the supply of new openings for them. Even those with technical skills will find themselves taking lesser jobs, while people who once would have occupied those positions drop off the bottom of the employment ladder.

In the first decades of extended life, the number of unemployed will soar. In the United States today, we hope to find jobs for perhaps 5 million working-age welfare recipients, and the truth is that for most of them no suitable openings are available. By 2020 or 2030, America alone will have as many as 50 million surplus job seekers to deal with. We do not see how productive work can be created for all who will need it.

The Great Depression of the 1930s showed us that not even the strongest nation can survive unless it provides a living for the great majority of its people. Yet the United States has already tried the traditional welfare model and concluded that unearned money corrodes the soul. Other lands have established even more paternalistic social systems and found them impossible to afford. We have considered schemes such as a negative income tax or a universal minimum income and found them wanting.

In the next thirty years, we are likely to require some new option, one that separates the need for a living wage from the requirement of traditional work, and does so without entirely abandoning our core values of productivity and self-reliance. The alternative could be a global return to private soup kitchens and government make-work programs on a scale not seen since the days of President Franklin Roosevelt, a full century earlier. Devising such a system may be the most difficult social challenge that arises during our extended lives. We have no idea how it will be met. We are certain only that it will be nearly impossible to avoid.

MODERNIZE THE BACKWARD LANDS

In today's world, it is not enough that the advanced industrial societies supply most of their own citizens with food and shelter, a sound education, and a rewarding career. The people of less developed lands require the same benefits if they are to survive in the tightly knit global economy of the next century. It is hard to deny that the rich lands have a moral obligation to help the poor ones; the duty of charity is stated or implied in virtually all of the world's religions and ethical structures. However, there are practical reasons to give development aid as well. In the postmortal age, the consequences of not providing for the poor nations could be so severe that the West will be unable to ignore the needs of its less fortunate neighbors.

The stakes are clearest in the Middle East, where the tensions between Israel and its neighbors are heightened by religious animosities of a virulence rarely seen in the West. For years, the entire region has been in a recession bordering on economic collapse. The poor have gathered in city slums where food, water, sanitation, and health care are scarce and hope is even more difficult to find. At one point, in Cairo, a city with an estimated population of more than 12 million, several hundred thousand people were living among, and even in, the crypts of a giant cemetery known as the City of the Dead. University graduates in Egypt once were guaranteed a job with the government or foreign corporations. More recently, their unemployment rate has hovered near 50 percent.

These problems are destined to get worse, not better. No fewer than 40 percent of the Arab people are under the age of 15. Their numbers will double by 2020, far outstripping any possible growth in the region's economy. Many young men are well educated, once members of a prosperous middle class, now poor and with no prospect of a better life. For some, fundamentalist faith is their only solace. The West, in their view, has not merely supported the hated Jewish state; both maliciously and by example, it has tempted Muslims away from pure Islam. That sense of aggrieved righteousness has made them ready prey for terrorist organizations in search of gullible candidates for suicide bombings and other dangerous missions.

Similar pools of disaffected, potentially violent young people are found wherever poverty is rife. In Latin America, terrorism is beginning to subside, but throughout the 1980s and early '90s, there were twice as many terrorist incidents involving Americans in Latin America each year as in the entire Muslim world. In the former Soviet Union, where poverty and ethnic hatred are no longer restrained by an overwhelming central government, terrorism also has begun to flourish. In Africa, tribal hatreds regularly erupt into war. In each region, futureless young provide the foot soldiers for insurrection. Given the right stimulus, they too could turn their attention toward the industrialized lands.

The changes soon to come can only make the world's poor angrier still. They will continue to live in poverty while even the most deprived people of the West enjoy comparative affluence. They will continue to die on nature's schedule, while those in richer lands live on. To many, this will seem to be more than unjust. It will appear to contravene the will of God. The Middle East at its most explosive has produced nothing like the wave of violence that life extension could inspire.

There is no guarantee that this particular nightmare will materialize, of course. Other factors could intervene to derail this grim scenario. Yet our best hope of averting chaos is to give the disaffected a stake in the future. Even the wealthy industrialized lands will find it difficult to jump-start the dormant economies of Africa and points east. It will be hard enough to pave the roads of the former Soviet Union, where an estimated 25 percent of the potato crop disappears en route to market simply because the ruts bounce the produce from the trucks. Harder still to build the roads that would carry food to remote corners of Africa or to supply schools and hospitals for all who need them. But probably necessary.

As we write this, we can hear cold-blooded planners in Western capitals respond: "Are they kidding? We'd have to spend ten billion dollars a year just to begin! What could terrorism cost us? A few hundred million? We can live with it. It's a no-brainer."

Perhaps so. It depends on our tolerance for the suffering of others, and for the suffering they may be willing to inflict upon us. The truth is that we have no hope of quickly improving the lot of all the world's poor. The job is too vast, the world's population is growing too quickly, and it is growing fastest in the lands where life is hardest. But we can make a start, and our own extended lives could be much easier if we are seen to try.

ENVIRONMENTAL IMPACT

Any change that increases the world's population automatically harms the environment. The more people there are, the more resources we will use and the more pollution we will generate. Nonetheless, there should be few environmental problems as a direct result of our prolonged lifespans. This first life-extended generation, the adults of the 1990s, amounts to no more than two hundred million people throughout the industrialized world. We can easily supply food, clothing, and shelter for them over the additional decades of their existence. Neither will doing so cause significant pollution. In a world of some 6 billion people, so few more will hardly be noticed.

(In this, we disagree with the Worldwatch Institute, which warns that the world's food supply soon will fall short of demand. It is true that some crop yields are declining, while the ocean's fisheries are being depleted. Yet we believe that other developments will offset any losses. Genetic engineering is one. The creation of crops for arid lands and brackish water, of disease-resistant plants, and of vegetables with longer shelf life will expand our food supply. Fish farming will make up for declining ocean catches. And irradiation of stored foods will stretch all the crops we grow. This process, a kind of super-Pasteurization, is used throughout the developed world, save in the United States, where it has been delayed by the same technophobes who once feared that microwave ovens would cause us to glow in the dark. Once the benefits and safety of irradiation are understood, it will be adopted as eagerly as microwaves were.)

Yet as an indirect result of life extension the planet could face severe environmental problems. The trouble comes when we try to deliver a better life to the world's poor. This requires not only food, clothing, and shelter, but electric lights and running water, refrigerators to keep food from spoiling, schools and hospitals, and roads to connect them all. And if the industrialized lands have only a few middle-aged adults to look after, the world at large is home to very many poor. Some 5.23 billion people (using 1996 population estimates) live in the 125 developing nations, and of these some 600 million live in the least developed countries of all—places like Eritrea, where the gross domestic product amounts to only $500 per capita and life expectancy at birth is only 50 years. Giving so many people even the minimum tolerable living standards will be an herculean task.

One nation shows the magnitude of this challenge. China, one of the more prosperous of the industrializing countries, is home to more than 1.2 billion people. Several years ago, Beijing stated its intent to produce a refrigerator for every household in the land. Unfortunately, China burns high-sulfur coal to generate most of its electricity. Scientists quickly calculated that producing and operating this one appliance for the world's most populous nation would soon double the planet's burden of greenhouse gasses. Global warming, if it has not already begun, would be inevitable.

China represents one-fifth of the world's population. Another three-fifths, more than 3 billion people, live in lands where standards of living are no better than China's and often are much worse.

If the global response to life extension prompts the rich lands to help their less well-to-do neighbors achieve a better standard of living, their efforts will help to mitigate the ultimate threat to Third World ecosystems. The challenge is to promote development without repeating the mistakes the industrial world has already made.

CONTROLLING POPULATION

In one respect, life extension should ease the world's population and environmental problems rather than aggravating them. If individuals live longer, the global birthrate should at last begin to subside and the burgeoning population come under control. And without that, progress on economic development and environmental protection will be all but impossible.

The world does not have too many people, but in many areas it is gaining more much more rapidly than it can provide for them. Between 1996 and 2026, the world's population will grow to nearly 8.3 billion. Virtually all of that growth will occur in the world's agrarian regions, where the only social security is a family in which younger members will grow up to support their parents' old age. The fertility rate in the developed regions averages only 1.7 children per woman. In the less developed lands, it rises to 3.3 children. And in the world's poorest nations, each woman delivers, on average, 5.4 children. Thus over the thirty years beginning in 1996, population in the developed regions is expected to grow by less than 6 percent; in Europe it will decline slightly. In the less developed nations, population will rise by 52 percent. In the least developed lands, it will soar by no less than 96 percent. Fully 98 percent of the world's population growth in the next three decades will occur in the countries that already find it difficult to support their people.

The environmental impact of this trend will be profound. Though agrarian societies do not generate the kinds of effluent thrown off by industrial economies, they clear-cut and burn forests for cropland, burn wood for fuel, generate greenhouse gases, and cause uncontrolled erosion of the denuded acreage. In the process, they destroy the habitat of endangered species. In Madagascar, unless deforestation can be halted, the famed lemur populations will be gone in twenty years. In other parts of Asia, the forests already have been burned.

By far the best hope of controlling environmental problems in the Third World lies with economic development. It is not merely a coincidence that as nations become wealthy, birthrates decline. One reason is that people who have the opportunity to buy consumer goods, to make their lives easier and more pleasant, often hesitate to sacrifice their immediate standard of living in order to support more children. Another is that better health care reduces mortality rates among the young, thus ensuring that most of a couple's children will survive to help them in old age. Most important of all, wealthier societies can afford to provide for their aged. When pensions and social security programs promise support late in life, they take over the most important practical role of adult offspring. Thus large families are no longer needed. Growing prosperity sometimes can lower fertility rates with surprising speed.

That will not be enough to satisfy the wealthy lands, however. In years past, international lenders such as the World Bank have debated adding a new condition to their loans—that borrower nations enact, and enforce, birth-control programs to reduce population growth. Politically and culturally, such schemes are anathema; religious conservatives of all three major faiths—Christianity, Judaism, and Islam—all vehemently reject birth control. Nonetheless, the idea makes practical sense. It is difficult enough to raise living standards in poor, unindustrialized lands. It becomes impossible when the population grows much faster than the local economy does.

To date, the nation most successful in slowing its population growth is China. It has accomplished this by enacting draconian restrictions on procreation. Chinese parents with one child face strong pressure not to have a second. Those with two are forbidden to have a third. Those who do have a third can no longer send their children to school, and they face other sanctions as well. There are exceptions for divorcées who want a second family and for parents whose child is significantly handicapped. Yet few societies could accept such intrusion by government into family life.

Nonetheless, we believe that international lenders eventually will require their client states to reduce their birthrates. Exploding populations simply waste too much of the development money they receive, and there is too little to go around as it is. Devising effective, acceptable population policies will be one more extremely difficult challenge for the life-extended world.

THE SEARCH FOR NEW MEANING

Our fifth and final challenge may be the most difficult of all, for it does not involve external circumstances but the core of our own being. It is a challenge that we all will have to meet, both as members of society and in the privacy of our own hearts. This is the search for purpose and meaning in a world where many of the old rules no longer apply. In a time when science has dramatically extended our lives, when it may even reduce death to a random accident that might strike us down at some point in the indefinable future, it will be necessary to figure out anew what is truly important to us and what may be set aside.

At the conscious level, most of us have long since set aside this kind of question. "The meaning of life" is a subject for the late-night debates of college sophomores, not the concern of responsible adults with children to raise and bills to pay. For some, the question may never have made all that much sense. Life simply is, to be lived in as much comfort and with as much pleasure as we can arrange while still meeting the obligations placed on us by society and our own ethical sense. These people may be the most sensible, best adjusted of all.

Yet there is another level, one at which no one can be immune to the existential questions about to be raised. Psychologists tell us that children are happy and secure only when they live within known and consistent limits. The boundaries set by our parents are an expression of their love, and they allow us to feel safe, much as cats relish the protection of small spaces. Without them, we grow up deformed, like the feral children too often seen on the nightly news. However, if all goes well, as we mature our borders recede in the external world, and we take the responsibility for living within them into our own hands. Adhering to the limits we know, we feel secure. Our ability to set aside questions of meaning simply shows how thoroughly we have absorbed our boundaries into the fiber of our own being.

There is no limit more absolute, nor more important, than the end of our lives. And if no healthy person welcomes it, nonetheless the finitude of life provides a framework for us, and a motive for our actions. Subconsciously, we measure our days along the imagined arc from birth to death and thereby give structure to what otherwise would be random existence. As Alan Harrington pointed out in *The Immortalist,* much that we do, however we rationalize our actions, originates in a disguised wish for the immortality of an afterlife. Without that impetus, it would lose most of its meaning. Much of mental illness, from classical depression to existential angst, originates when that sense of meaning fails us.

In the next twenty years or so, the most important of the borders that give our lives meaning will recede into the unknowable future. Effective immortality will not be the stuff of a theoretical afterlife but a real possibility carrying the scientific seal of approval. A fence on which we leaned without even knowing it will have collapsed under us, and it may seem that life provides neither limits nor security. Picture yourself as an astronaut untethered, surrounded by the infinite depths of space and gripped by the sense that you are falling endlessly toward Earth's unyielding surface hundreds of miles below. We may not even understand what is wrong, but the wrongness of it will affect us nonetheless.

We do not mean to suggest that life without the certainty of a predictable death will be a moral void. Yet the foundation of our existence, our sense of meaning, must undergo a profound shift. Where once we accepted boundaries forced on us from outside, we will have to build new ones, beginning with fundamental values that we may never have examined rigorously. This is a challenge like none that most of us have ever faced.

For some, the triumph of aging research, the transition to something that may approach limitless life, will be scarcely noticed. Buffered by deep religious faith, intellectual preoccupation, or a rare, unshakable sense of security, they will move unruffled into their extended lives. Others may be so disoriented that they require psychiatric help to find values and goals to carry them through the extra decades. A few may examine their options and decide to forgo extended life, concluding that they prefer the brief years that nature, or their God, granted them; we know one couple already who have already made that choice. Yet hardly any will find themselves entirely unchanged.

We cannot begin to predict where artificially prolonged life will lead us. In the end, we believe the discovery of age-preventing therapies will be a net gain for humanity. Thus far, this is largely a matter of our own faith. But it now seems very likely that we ourselves will be here to see the results. And we have begun to ponder the value and meaning of our own extended lives.

HOME AND HOSPICE CARE FOR THE PERIMORTAL AGE

Thus far, we have dealt with the future more speculatively than we normally would. We have felt justified in taking this unconventional approach because of the enormous impact that any significant advance in life extension will have on all our lives. If there were only one chance in ten that science would soon extend the human life span beyond its expected limits, that possibility still would demand our immediate attention. As we have seen, any such fundamental transformation would so change both society and our personal lives that we cannot afford to let it come upon us unaware. No area of human activity will be more affected than home and hospice care. And, for the reasons outlined in Chapter 1, we believe the chances that anti-aging research will radically prolong our lives within the foreseeable future are much better than one in ten.

However, the impact of this development remains many years off. It could take a decade or more to prove the value of anti-aging therapies so conclusively that they are widely adopted in the developed countries. After that, the senior population would begin to grow, but it would take still more years for the effects to be felt. Assuming that many people have taken to melatonin, or whatever therapy eventually proves successful, by 2010, it will still be 2020 before the senior population has grown enough, and grown healthy enough, to change the market for care. It will be 2030 before the full extent of this transformation is known.

Thus we wish to devote the next few pages to health care in the "perimortal" period, the time of uncertainty that we now appear to be entering, when the prospect of life extension clearly lies before us, but the reality is still some distance off. During these years, we must prepare for the transition to come. It will be difficult enough to cope with the forces already changing the environment for providers of home and hospice care.

The next ten years at least will be a time of growing demand for the services of home care and hospice providers, but also a time of growing constraints. The senior population will grow rapidly, but it is likely to become healthier as well. Third-party payers will grow more willing to underwrite any service that promises to reduce the overall cost of patient care, but an expanding share of the nation's health care will be handled through managed-care systems. The trend toward providing high-tech health care in the home setting can only grow, but there will be a shortage of trained, or even trainable, personnel to perform new and complex therapeutic procedures. And at all times, for all providers, the demand to cut costs and prove the value of all services delivered will be a constant pressure on management and caregivers alike. The early twenty-first century will be a rewarding period for home care and hospice services, but it will be a challenging one as well.

BASIC ASSUMPTIONS

In looking at the future of home and hospice care, we inevitably have made some assumptions about the world in general, the context within which these industries will grow and operate. It seems only sensible to spell them out before moving on to their implications. We have identified twelve crucial assumptions that will affect home care, and ten corollaries that seem to flow inevitably from them.

- There will be sharp and continuing growth in the number of senior citizens in the developed lands, who will in turn face an increasing number of diseases and disabilities. Among the most prominent and fastest-growing ills are cancer, heart disease, stroke, arthritis, diabetes, and Alzheimer's disease.
- Technology will continue to extend our lives. Among the most

significant developments of the next decade will be gene therapy; new cancer treatments, probably including a general cure
for cancer; new forms of hormone replacement; and possibly
rejection-free organ transplants.

- Technology will make it possible to deliver more and more
  health-care services at home. These include IVs, telemedicine
  delivery (monitoring devices, EKGs, etc.), more convenient
  monitoring of sugar and cholesterol levels for diabetics and
  heart patients, on-site urinalysis, occult blood screening, special
  beds, and closed-circuit alarm systems. These will improve both
  patient survival and quality of life.

- Demand for home and hospice care will grow rapidly. Several
  factors lead to this assumption. The Baby Boom generation, 77
  million strong, is quickly reaching the age at which medical
  needs grow. Because of growing work demands and large geographic separations, it is becoming more difficult to travel to
  care for infirm parents. For similar reasons, it takes too much
  time to visit institutionalized parents. And hospice patients prefer to remain at home as long as possible. Some 16 percent arrive at the hospice less than a week before death. One in four die
  within two weeks after acceptance, and half die within one
  month.

- Home care will continue to enjoy the support of federal, state,
  and local policy-makers. Home care costs only one-third as
  much as institutional care, it keeps families together, and consumers (and voters) prefer it.

- Managed care will affect the delivery of home care until the
  turn of the century. The demand for cost reduction, the growing number of managed-care consumers, tighter regulation,
  and the potential for a conflict of values all will affect this trend.

- Paraprofessional services will grow. There will be more physician assistants, more practical nurses, more home orderlies,
  more post-retirement helpers, and more computer-savvy Generation Xers to assist.

- There will be less pressure from labor unions. Union membership dropped from 23.6 percent of workers in 1980 to 11.2 percent in 1995. By 2000, less than 10 percent of workers will be

union members. Only half of unionized workers will have the power to strike. The others will be federal, state, county, or municipal workers who are forbidden by law to go on strike. That means that only 5 percent of the workers in the United States will be able to walk off the job by 2000.

- Private insurance will supply more revenue for home-care services. Generation Xers already are buying their own policies. Retirement-age individuals are buying private policies to pay for home care. Baby Boomers are witnessing the difficulties of underinsured parents and will be better prepared themselves.

- . Private buyers also will contribute more revenue to home care. Older individuals will use their private funds for home care, rather than paying more for institutional care. Generation Xers will save their own money over a longer period to pay for their own care, rather than relying on Medicare to pay their way.

- More co-payments will be available for medicine. The recent federal budget-balancing agreement counts on co-payments to take up a greater part of this burden. Both parties have accepted the need to increase co-payments over the next five years.

- Medicare revenue will flatten out. Recalculation of the Consumer Price Index will reduce Medicare payments. Eventually, Medicare will be means-tested; those who make too much will not be covered.

- Regulatory contraints will grow.

- Aggregate dollars spent for both health care and home care will continue to grow, but at a slower rate than in the past.

- States will exercise greater control over Medicaid.

- Both vertical and horizontal consolidation of the health-care industry will continue.

- More home-health agencies will be affiliated with hospitals or managed-care systems.

- Staff functions increasingly will be outsourced and privatized.

- The home-care industry will be seeing a growing number of acutely sick patients.

- Nontraditional services will make up a growing part of home-care practice.

- Information systems will give consumers greater control over health-care decisions affecting them, their families, and their loved ones.

- Patients, who now arrive by referral from primary-care physicians and hospitals, will increasingly choose their own home-care and hospice services.

MARKET FORCES

Clearly the single most important factor in the future of home and hospice care in the United States is the growth of the senior population. Between 1990 and 2000, the over-65 population of the United States will have grown by nearly 3.5 million, from 31.2 million people to 34.7 million. In the decade that follows, the country will gain another 4.8 million seniors. By 2020, when most of the Baby Boom generation have at last reached retirement age, the senior population will rise to 53.2 million, a leap of more than 53 percent in a single decade.

Among this group, the oldest subset is growing most quickly. Those over age 85 made up only 3 million people in 1990, or 1.2 percent of the population. By 2010, this will rise by 90 percent, to 5.7 million. Twenty years later, as the Baby Boomers are entering this final stage of life, the number of people over age 85 will reach 8.5 million, or 2.4 percent of the population. The number will not peak until at least 2050, when 4.6 percent of Americans, more than 18.2 million people, have joined these "oldest old."

We find similar trends throughout most of the world. Among the member countries of the Organization for Economic Cooperation and Development, 18 percent of people were over age 60 in 1990. By 2030, they will make up more than 30 percent of the population. The over-80 group, now about 3 percent of the population, will double. In the Netherlands, a reasonably typical European population, the number of people over age 65 will rise from 13 percent of the population today to more than 22 percent in 2050. In China, the fraction of people over 60 will rise from less than 10 percent now to about 22 percent in 2030. In Japan, where life expectancies are the highest in the world, 13 percent of the population, some 16.2 million people, were age 65 or older in 1992. By 2025, when the proportion of elderly in Japan is expected to peak, this figure will increase to nearly 26 percent. Only in Africa, where life still is comparatively brief, will the proportion of elderly remain stable.

As populations age, their health needs will rise quickly. In the United States, our individual medical bills triple between our early 30s and our early 50s, from about $1,500 per year on average to $4,500. At the age of 40, most Americans already must live with at least one chronic illness. By age 85, people report an average of four separate disabilities. Again, this mirrors experience throughout the developed lands. In Japan, which is generally the healthiest of the major trading nations, the fraction of people reporting symptoms of chronic illness is about 50 percent at age 65—44 percent for men, 51 percent among women.

All this argues for extremely rapid growth in hospice care, for the most significant death rate will not change—one person, one death. However, new medical technologies will slightly retard the growth of home health care. Over the next twenty years, the treatment of chronic diseases will undergo a transformation comparable to the introduction of antibiotics in the 1930s. By the time Baby Boomers reach their 70s, "antisense" drugs will be used to inhibit the defective RNA and DNA that are ultimately responsible for cancers, Alzheimer's disease, and autoimmune disorders such as rheumatoid arthritis. Gene-transfer therapies will be well on their way toward eliminating most hereditary diseases. Tissue implants and "tissue engineering" will be used to cure diabetes, amyotrophic lateral sclerosis, arthritis, and many other pathologies. It seems likely that even heart disease and stroke will come under reliable medical control.

In the United States, the revolution in personal habits which began in the 1970s also will improve health in the early twenty-first century. By 2000, the proportion of smokers in the American population will be only half what it was at the peak in the 1950s. At the same time, the rate of consumption of red meats, fatty foods, and alcohol has dropped precipitously, while the number of people reporting regular exercise has climbed rapidly. Thus, emphysema, chronic obstructive pulmonary disease, coronary artery disease, and many other disorders typical of later life are coming under control.

All this is resulting in a compression of morbidity, in which people experience fewer symptoms of chronic disease and disability, and those symptoms are delayed till later in life. According to a study at Duke University, the number of older Americans reporting disabilities has already begun to drop, most likely because of improved health habits over the last twenty years. Some 7.1 million Americans were at least partially disabled in 1994, down from the 8.3 million that would have been expected based on the rates seen only twelve years earlier. As the Baby Boom generation reaches its senior years, these benefits will be felt even more strongly. Thus the demand for home health care will not grow quite as rapidly as simple aging data suggest.

Note that the dramatic change in health-related habits is strictly an American phenomenon. In Europe, smoking and dietary habits remain unchanged, while throughout the rest of the world smoking and excessively rich diets are becoming more common rather than less so. Thus we can expect to see a much smaller improvement in senior-years health in Europe than in the United States. In Asia, Africa, and Latin America, life expectancies will continue to rise owing to the growing availability of medical care, but morbidity in later life will increase, just as it did in the United States for most of this century.

Throughout the developed world, economic factors will promote the growth of home health care. As national medical bills have risen, the pressure to limit them has grown. This is particularly true in the United States, where the establishment of Medicare and Medicaid was not accompanied by significant controls on the growth of health spending. Thus, with the growth of managed-care programs, hospital patients are being discharged "quicker and sicker." The task of overseeing the recovery of these patients has fallen largely to home-care services. This role can only expand as the crisis in health-care funding grows more acute.

In all, the growth in the elderly population, combined with the demand to provide care in the most economically efficient manner possible, guarantees the rapid growth of home health care for at least the next fifteen years. Between 1995 and 2010, the demand for home medical services could easily double.

A CHANGING ENVIRONMENT

At least four factors will complicate the task of meeting that demand. These are a widespread trend that we call "bimodal distribution," the arrival of competition for the home-care market, the growing sophistication of services provided at home, and the tightening labor market in the United States.

In a wide variety of industries, economic pressures are promoting the growth of large corporations and chains, and also of small operators. At one end of the markets from banking to farming, economies of scale give the giants an unbeatable advantage. At the other, niche markets provide lucrative footholds for tiny, tightly focused "boutiques." Yet midsized competitors, enjoying neither advantage, are squeezed out. Thus giant hospital chains absorb their smaller competitors or drive them out of business, and local health clinics thrive, but regional chains are fast disappearing. Small drug retailers struggle to survive in a world of thousand-store chains, while the best-managed local stores—but only the best-managed—hold their own.

As the demand for cost-efficient health care grows ever more strident, economic and regulatory pressure will promote much the same bimodal distribution among home-health and hospice services. In the major urban and suburban markets, local and regional providers will quickly be aggregated into centrally managed chains with vast purchasing power and low administrative costs. By 2010, we expect freestanding services to be most viable in rural areas and in those dense, relatively poor inner-city neighborhoods that profit-oriented providers will view as less attractive markets.

Complicating the problems of today's home-care services will be the growth of two relatively new competitors. Assisted-living facilities now provide much the same services as home-health-care agencies. Some are allied with hospitals and can supply comprehensive care, even in time of acute illness. At least a few offer terminal care as well. They have proved popular among the well-to-do elderly who can afford premium service, and especially among those who have few nearby relatives to help out with daily needs. At the same time, health maintenance organizations and other prepaid managed-care systems are entering the field. This allows them both to retain whatever profit is to be made from home care and to control the quantity and quality of services delivered to outpatients.

Those services are increasingly sophisticated. Blood-glucose monitoring, pump-driven tube feedings, wound care, automated peritoneal dialysis, and many other services once limited to the hospital and office setting are today routinely performed at home. In the future, these will include diagnostic and therapeutic procedures involving automated blood analyses, overseeing the results of genetic and drug therapies, and computerized health monitoring. Recruiting and training personnel to take on these roles will be a growing challenge for health-service managers in the next decade.

In fact, it will not be easy to find enough caregivers to provide even basic service. As the Baby Boom generation has reached economic maturity, it has left such demanding yet relatively low-paid fields to its offspring. And there are not many of them. The declining birthrates since the 1960s mean that the supply of workers is shrinking rapidly. The key 18-to-34 age group has already shrunk from 28 percent of the American population in 1990 to about 24 percent and will decline to 23 percent by 2010. This does not sound like a great change, but in a growing economy it will prove critical. Home care will find itself particularly affected, because it takes one caregiver to serve each patient. As Baby Boomers increasingly need health services, the ratio of new workers to care for them will be much less than one-to-one. Home-care and hospice agencies will find that they must make do with fewer and less well educated workers, even as they are forced to pay more to hire and train them.

In this environment, employee relations will be a major concern. Merely retaining skilled caregivers in a competitive labor market will require that personnel feel their efforts are both well compensated and well appreciated. The declining fortunes of labor unions make this concern especially acute. In recent years, unions

have been forced to search for new members outside their traditional industries. Health-care workers represent one of the more
attractive markets in which they can hope to win recruits. They
must feel that they are treated fairly and paid competitively. Otherwise, unionization could have a major impact on this industry in the
years to come.

DOING MORE WITH LESS

In this Darwinian environment, where every health-care dollar
counts and competition is growing rapidly, home-care and hospice
providers must pursue a variety of strategies to ensure their continued prosperity. Anything that can be done to reduce costs, maintain patient satisfaction, justify existing services, develop new ones,
and open new markets is not merely desirable, but mandatory.

For several years now, home-health-care agencies have felt pres-
sured to form alliances with managed-care systems. The alternative
has been to face the loss of referral sources. Yet many recent studies
have suggested that this is only a temporary phenomenon—that as
soon as 2000, and surely no later than 2005, patients will select their
own home-care providers, using the Internet to shop for the service
that best meets their needs. We very much doubt that this will happen. Many new users of computerized information services quickly
find that they must cut back their online hours so as to preserve time
for normal daily life. Even experienced Net users often complain of
information overload. It will take much longer than many observers
imagine for people to integrate online services so completely into
their lives that they use them for such personal needs as selecting a
home-care provider. The majority of today's seniors, and even many
Baby Boomers, may never make the transition. Instead, they will
continue to rely on doctors—the ultimate authority figures—and
hospital personnel to make the choice for them. In cities and the
more populous suburbs, home-care and hospice agencies must cultivate whatever alliances they can with managed-care systems. That
requirement will not change in the next five years, and probably
not in the next ten.

The National Association for Home Care has united several useful measures into its NAHC Plus program. Combining the needs of NAHC members into a group purchasing plan will help independent home-care and hospice providers to gain the economies of scale formerly available only to much larger organizations. Making financial services available at modest rates to members in times of economic stress also is another step in this direction. NAHC's proposed "home-care university" could go a long way toward solving the problem of finding and training employees in the tight labor market for home-health-care workers in the early twenty-first century. Hospices, in contrast, are not likely to solve their labor problem. People who can withstand the emotional rigors of providing close personal care to the dying will always be in short supply.

The availability of caregivers trained in both sophisticated medical procedures and old-fashioned dedication to personal attention in turn will promote a high level of patient satisfaction. This is critical for independent providers, whose reputation for personal care will help them to prosper in an age that often favors large organizations and a "least-common-denominator" approach to services and marketing.

Information technology offers many other opportunities to improve and streamline health care. Both to guarantee their own efficiency and to justify their work to reimbursement sources, home-care agencies in particular must be able to define what can be expected from their efforts and to demonstrate the value and quality of each visit. This means gathering and collating large quantities of information about the cost and benefits of services provided. Home-care operators will have to develop more sophisticated ways of collecting and manipulating data as competition in health care grows.

At first glance, this appears less an issue for hospices, where patient outcome is known by definition. Patients are not admitted to a hospice unless their physicians have certified that they have less than six months to live and patient and next of kin have agreed that no heroic measures will be used to prolong their lives. According to figures reported in early 1997, fully 16 percent of hospice patients die within the first week of their stay, 25 percent within two weeks, and 50 percent within a month. Under the circumstances, it is difficult to see how to measure service to hospice patients. Yet careful attention to costs and documentation of service to the patient's family are the only objective data that can substantiate the value of hospice care. We believe that developing clear, quantifiable criteria for their performance will be one of the more difficult and important challenges for hospices in the near future.

Computerized information systems also present the chance to develop wholly new services. In ten years, wristwatch-sized monitors will relay patient data via telephone or computer network directly to the home-care office. This will allow twenty-four-hour monitoring of such critical functions as blood pressure, heartbeat, and even insulin level, with instant response in case of emergency. Health-coaching software will help patients to maintain diets, exercise regimens, and medication schedules. And networked computers will allow providers to make "video house calls" to check in on patients between in-person visits. All these services will make for better health care and at the same time tighten the bond between patient and provider.

New services and new approaches to existing services will be a major part of home care in the coming decade. Telemonitoring is only one of them. As chronic illness and disability decline among seniors, other needs will gain greater prominence. As managed-care systems discharge patients earlier, home-care providers have taken on the role of overseeing convalescence from acute care among patients of all age groups. This will be one of the fastest-growing segments of home care in the years to come. For older patients, home-care agencies may provide slightly less in the way of physical medicine, but much more social and psychological care. In a time of rapid change, these services will be in high demand.

As medical technologies become more sophisticated and widely available, another need is likely to appear. Ten years from now, the entire human genome will have been mapped, and many of its medically significant functions will be known. Physicians will be able to test for most or all genetic disorders and disease susceptibilities early in life, often years before they have any effect on the patient's health. Individuals who can expect eventually to develop a significant illness, such as cancer, will need to be monitored regularly for evidence of the disease. This is a natural role for home care. Many work-related illnesses also involve some inherited susceptibility. At the moment, it seems that employers probably will be banned from discriminating against job applicants based on genetic data. Thus they will be eager to watch at-risk employees for any sign of medical problems. Home-care providers are the most obvious candidates to manage these monitoring programs.

For larger, profit-oriented providers, the most obvious growth opportunities lie overseas. In Eastern Europe and Asia particularly, large and growing senior populations combine with newly prosperous economies to create a strong demand for health care in all its forms. As Latin America gains in economic and social stability, it too will become an attractive market for home-health and hospice services. These developing economies thus far are less competitive than those of the United States, Canada, and Western Europe. Providers who enter them in the next decade will be well positioned to benefit from their continuing growth.

CARE FOR A POSTMORTAL AGE

Here we return to speculation for the long term. Yet it is speculation of such a fundamental nature that we consider it necessary. Recent claims that readily available hormones such as melatonin, DHEA, and pregnenolone can improve our health and extend our lives seem overblown. At the least, they are poorly substantiated. Yet the fundamental research that inspired these promises appears to be sound. It may well result in practical ways to extend the human life span during the natural lives of the Baby-Boom generation. These treatments can be expected to bring a life expectancy of 110 to 115 years, preserving our health and vigor almost to the end of our lives.

Several antiaging treatments have already been demonstrated in the laboratory. Animals receiving them rarely suffer the diseases that otherwise are common in old age. They remain healthy until the end of their lives, then die without warning or identifiable cause. This may well be the future we can expect for ourselves. If current research pans out, heart disease, cancer, stroke, diabetes, arthritis, and almost any other chronic illness will become as uncommon, and probably as treatable and transitory, as infectious diseases are today.

If this is even conceivable, it is a prospect of such importance that it must be anticipated and strategies devised to deal with it. We believe that it is more than conceivable. The chance that current research will lead to a significant extension of human life spans appears easily to reach the range of 50 percent by 2010 and close to inevitable in the decade after that.

In this very possible future, hospices will still be needed, because everyone still will die; in this respect only the schedule will have changed. Hospice service may even become more important, both to patients and to their families, because the end of life will arrive with comparatively little warning. There will be few chronic disabilities or prolonged illnesses to accustom people to the idea that death is near. Thus, comfort and emotional support will be all the more important in a life-extended world.

For home-care services, the prospect is altogether different. Chronic disease and disability will not be unknown, but they will no longer be the rule. Home care late in life will be limited to a brief transition period before the patient enters a hospice. Instead, home care will come to specialize in the novel services described above: social and psychological support, convalescence from acute care— quite possibly for a leg broken on the ski slope at the age of 95—monitoring of potential genetic problems, and providing individually tailored advice about health practices. For profit-oriented providers, overseas markets will become dramatically more important, for life extension is unlikely to reach less developed countries for years after it has transformed the United States.

There is another possibility, however. Life extension might reduce one role for home care, but add a new and even more important one. Though very simple regimens have proved to extend the lives of laboratory animals, human beings may well require treatments tailored to individual needs. Home-care services would be ideally suited to monitor patients' hormone levels and adjust dosages on a continuing basis. If it turns out that each of us requires his or her own unique anti-aging "cocktail," home-care providers could soon find themselves supplying a key service to every household in the developed world. We believe this is a very real possibility.

SOURCE DOCUMENT

Much of the preceding analysis was based on the results of a questionnaire prepared by Forecasting International and sent to leaders in the fields of home and hospice care. That questionnaire is reproduced below. Following each question is one typical answer. These answers were given by Marylin Dean, R.N., M.P.H., B.S.N., National Director of Home Care Services for Interim Healthcare, one of the most respected suppliers of home care in the United States.

Home and Hospice Care in the Early Twenty-first Century

Long-term care in all its forms faces a turbulent, but perhaps rewarding, future. Advances in the treatment of heart disease, cancer, and other such ills have combined with improved diet and fitness to increase the number of people who survive into old age, and thus need care for chronic disorders. At the same time, political and economic pressures are demanding that patients receive the most cost-effective care possible; in many cases, this is care at home or in a hospice, rather than in a traditional hospital or nursing home. By 2010, the giant Baby Boom generation will begin to reach their retirement years; in the decades that follow, all else being equal, they will provide a growing demand for medical care of all kinds. However, research is attacking the diseases of old age, and success in these efforts could significantly reduce the need of the elderly for medical care. There even is evidence that research into the aging process could dramatically improve our vigor and resistance to disease late in life. This combination of conflicting trends make it uncommonly difficult to predict the market for health care even for a few years into the future.

Our purpose in this questionnaire is to assess the expectations of professionals in the fields of home-health and hospice care. These forecasts will be used to develop a baseline model of the industry against which to examine possible developments over the next twenty years. We hope that respondents will elaborate their answers, providing hard numbers wherever possible, discussing their views, and explaining the reasons behind them as comprehensively as busy schedules allow. These are intended as essay questions, not true/false!

Thank you for your help in this project.

1. In many industries, we have observed what we call "the bimodal distribution of institutions." That is, giant banks, agribusinesses, and hospital chains prosper. Small banks, farms, and hospitals survive by concentrating on giving the best possible service to niche markets. However, midsized generalists either die out or are absorbed by their larger competitors.

   • To what extent will this trend affect home health care and hospices?

   • Will most home-health and hospice providers be linked into regional or national chains five, ten, or twenty years from now? Or will they retain their separate, local identities?

   Large chains will be prevalent. Midsize providers will survive based upon customer satisfaction and a good reputation for excellent patient care.

   EXAMPLE: Midsize agency specializing in pediatric home care that has caregiver specialists and expertise. Such agencies will continue to grow because of need. If physicians and their patients are satisfied with the service, they will be okay. Managed care will have a large play in determining who will get the business, which will make it hard for the small agencies unless they have excellent customer satisfaction.

2. Assisted-living facilities now provide the same services as home-health-care agencies, and at least a few offer terminal care. They have proved popular among the well-to-do elderly who can afford this premium service.

   • To what extent will these other innovations in health-care delivery affect the home-health-care and hospice industry?

- In what ways?
- Will assisted-living facilities co-opt wealthier patients, leaving home and hospice service for patients less able to pay for service?
- Can hospices form alliances to provide terminal care for these new competitors?

Assisted Living

Assisted-living facilities are a good answer for elderly who have no willing or able family or significant other to help in their care. As the population grows older, there will be more of a need for assisted living and/or home care.

EXAMPLE: Elderly woman with family living in other areas of the country and needing help with activities of daily living. Too feeble to shop, put away groceries, cook, etc., and no regular person to help with these tasks. Assisted living will help all to assure the safety and social needs of this person. However, home care and companion care will be able to assist a primary caregiver with the necessary tasks.

Payment for Services

Most patients prefer to be at home, and that is the choice they do make. The wealthier client will be able to afford to remain at home. Reimbursement by outside sources and insurance companies will help to allow patients to remain in their homes, but that is a new concept for the non-Medicare-reimbursed and patients with chronic illness. Current legislation being presented looks at certain chronic illness and ways to provide care.

3. The current federal effort at health-care reform aims to reduce the national medical bill by promoting managed care and other cost-effective delivery systems. It seems likely that reimbursement will be extended to home care, assisted-living facilities, and other providers formerly left out. However, there will be less money per capita to divide between these levels of health care.
    - In general, how do you believe these changes will play out for home care and hospices?

- How many of the patients now receiving hospital or outpatient care could reasonably be discharged to home care?
- To what extent can home-care providers and hospices form working alliances with managed-care systems?
- Overall, will the industry benefit or suffer from the effort to trim health care costs?

Managed Care and Cost-Efficient Care

Home-care agencies will have to run efficiently and be able to present measurable outcomes to the reimbursement sources. It will not be enough to predict how many visits will be needed; agencies will also need to show what will be done during each visit and what can be expected as a result of the care given. Efficient agencies with ability to show outcomes will fare well.

Interim has a system called InterPath, which documents home visits and expected outcomes by disease. This system is used to track patient care and to collect outcome information. This information can be given back to the reimbursement sources to demonstrate the value and quality of each visit.

4. Increasingly sophisticated technologies are finding their way out of the hospital and into outpatient clinics and home-care services. These include blood-glucose monitoring, pump-driven tube feedings, automated peritoneal dialysis, and other services formerly limited to inpatient settings. Many more such developments will inevitably appear in the years to come.
    - How, and how significantly, will they change the nature of home care in the next two decades?

New Technology and Home Care

High-tech care is currently being done in the home. IVs, tests, wound care, etc. are being done after surgery, but Medicare only pays for care to those who are homebound and unable to go to a physician's office for care. There is a need for home services to be routinely provided to patients who are returning to the home quicker but sicker. Many do not understand the medications and treatments they are expected to provide for themselves. Telephone monitoring to support them can reduce costs and still assure safe follow-up care. This will be very important when there is not a willing and able caregiver available. Disease prevention will be high priority for all health-care organizations.

There will be a demand for more qualified workers who can provide the high-tech care safely and correctly. In addition, with the growing number of Alzheimer's patients there will be a need for caregivers who understand their needs and are able to cope with the confused, difficult patient at home. This will also require training personnel.

Opportunities

Creative methods and ways to provide services will need to be devised. Again, telemonitoring will be used. Families and other community resources will be necessary to provide the assistance needed to enable the patient to remain at home.

5. Growing shortages of trained personnel have affected health services in many regions of the United States.
   - Will home-care and hospice agencies have the personnel they need to meet the demand for their services in five, ten, or twenty years?
   - Will they have, or be able to train, workers capable of administering the sophisticated technologies mentioned in Question 4?
   - Will they be able to afford the higher wages and benefits these workers are likely to demand?

As home care requires a one-to-one ratio, there will continue to be a need for more personnel. This profession/vocation will need to be marketed in order to attract caring workers. Second-career workers or those returning to the workforce after their children are grown will be key targets for additional workers. Training, orientation, and ongoing supervision/support for the workers will be key to keeping them in this field.

Home-care agencies will find it necessary to change their current methods of getting workers. Training will be very important, and retention will be critical.

Obtaining workers to provide the high-tech care will be a challenge. Families and significant others will need to be taught how to monitor and assist with the care. Schools need to be preparing workers to provide care in the home. The nursing programs are slow to offer the home-care segment.

Higher Wages and Benefits

All will have to work more efficiently, and there will be a need to have creative methods of payment from reimbursement sources to meet the needs for home care. This will prevent the more expensive alternatives, such as longer hospital stays.

6. Health-care workers represent one of the more attractive groups in which labor unions can hope to recruit new members.
    *   Will unionization have a major impact on home care and hospices?
    *   What can the industry do to forestall or adapt to unionization?
    All the principles of why workers join a union will come into play. If workers are happy and feel a part of the organization, there will be less chance for the union to enter. There is always a possibility of this occurring.
    It will be necessary to have satisfied, happy workers who feel they are treated fairly and are paid competitive wages.

7. Seniors, and particularly those over age 85, who traditionally require the most medical care, now form the fastest-growing demographic group in the United States and other developed countries. By 2010, the Baby Boom generation will enter its years of highest demand for health services. Thus, virtually all current forecasts predict a dramatic growth in the number of patients requiring chronic care in all its forms.
    *   To what extent do these commonsense forecasts influence your own expectations for the future of the home-care and hospice industry?
    *   To what extent will the growing tendency of older Americans to be divorced, single, separated, or childless increase the need for home and hospice care?
    With the increasing numbers of elderly, the need for care in the home will also increase. Agencies will need to set goals and develop measurable

outcomes and expectations for care. Volunteers need to be utilized in conjunction with services to meet some of the nonphysical needs of the patients. All will need to be creative and think "out of the box."

The number of of those over 85 living alone will increase. Education and disease prevention will be a key to keeping them healthy and independent as long as possible. Support services will be needed to enable them to stay home as long as possible. All will need to take more accountability for their own health and avoid unhealthy lifestyles.

8. Though the elderly seem likely to remain the dominant users of home and hospice care, younger persons with chronic and medically complex conditions also seem likely to need these services. These include AIDS patients and others.
   - To what extent will they augment the market for home and hospice care?
   - How well are home-care and hospice providers prepared to meet their needs?
   - What can be done to serve these patients better?

Large numbers of AIDS patients, pediatric patients, and medically complex patients currently receive care in the home. The public is becoming more aware of home care, and demands are being made on physicians to offer it to patients.

Serving Patients Better

There will continue to be a large need to educate physicians on the benefits of home care and the ways to monitor patients in the home.

Reimbursement is always an issue. There is a large segment of the population uncovered for necessary service. All will need to be educated on the cost-effectiveness of the use of home care. Legislators will continue to need to be shown the benefits of home care and how it will reduce the cost of institutionalization and provide for a happier population.

9. Biomedical researchers are striving to cure, or at least mitigate, many of the diseases that most commonly require home care. In recent months, they have announced tantalizing breakthroughs in their understanding of such disorders as arthritis, osteoporosis, and even

Alzheimer's disease. It seems likely that at least some of these theoretical developments will lead to effective new clinical treatments during the period under study.

- To what extent will new therapies reduce the need for home and hospice care?
- Will other developments compensate for this potential loss of market by opening home care to patients who now require hospitalization? To what extent?

Activities of daily living will continue to be a need for all elderly patients. The aging process will continue, and patients are getting older. There will be an increased need for paraprofessional services at home. Again, education for the public on prevention of disease and healthy lifestyles and also the appeal to potential workers to enter the home-care field will be critical.

10. In the last eighteen months, several popular books have promised readers that taking such readily available hormones as melatonin, DHEA, and pregnenolone could improve their health and even extend their lives. The fundamental research that inspired these claims appears to be sound. There is a nonnegligible possibility that it will lead to practical interventions in human aging within the period covered by this study. If begun at the age of 40, they could be expected to extend the human life span to roughly 115 years. Those who began treatment later in life could expect lesser, but still substantial, benefits.

Animals receiving such therapies rarely suffer the diseases that otherwise afflict them during old age. They remain healthy until the end of their lives, then die without warning or obvious cause. Most scientists working in this field assume that their research eventually will provide much the same benefits for human beings. Within twenty years, this could dramatically reduce the incidence of cancer, heart disease, arthritis, and the many other diseases commonly associated with advancing years.

- How can providers of home or hospice care prepare to face this potential change in their expectations?
- What other roles can home and hospice services take on if their traditional function declines?

There will continue to be a need for social and psychological needs to be met. Companion-homemaker services as well as nurse-aide services will continue to grow. Need for assistance with activities of daily living will continue. There will also be a need for high-tech services for those who do get sick. Patients will continue to die and need hospice services to assist both the patient and the family. Preventive services will be increased to enable patients to remain at home and out of expensive institutions.

SEVENTY-FOUR TRENDS FOR A POSTMORTAL AMERICA

GENERAL LONG-TERM SOCIETAL TRENDS

1. The United States will remain prosperous throughout the fore-seeable future. Widespread affluence, low interest rates, low inflation, and low unemployment—both in real numbers and as a percentage of the workforce—will be the norm for at least the next fifteen years.

    *   Economic growth will benefit from improved manufacturing technology, which boosts productivity and reduces the unit cost of goods. At the same time, slow growth in the labor force will be offset by workers who remain on the job longer. Thus, both prices and wages are likely to remain under control.
    *   From 2011 onward, when workers in the Baby Boom generation would have been expected to retire, and then to die off, the continued presence of life-extended workers in the job market will begin to disrupt this baseline economic forecast. Interest and inflation rates will remain low. Nonetheless, affluence will begin to erode as the supply of workers—already more than we need—begins to grow even more quickly than the economy can absorb them and the Gross National Product must be shared among more people.
    *   American companies today are giving more overtime and hiring more part-time employees than at any time in the past twenty years. This appears to represent a permanent change

in business practices. Full-time hiring may rebound temporarily if life extension is delayed for a few years, so that the first Baby Boomers begin to retire and only smaller generations are available to replace them. However, the current trend will reassert itself when life-extended Boomers either return to the labor market or decide never to leave it.

- Life extension will speed the expected improvement in productivity. Manufacturing efficiency depends not just on technology but on the availability of capital to pay for it. Older people own most of society's capital, because they have had more time to amass it and because their political power has skewed laws in their favor. They also are the most likely to invest in the stocks and bonds that supply money for investment in new productive capacity. Longer lives will allow them to gather an even greater share of the nation's resources, which in turn will be reinvested in productive ways.

- Note that this growing concentration of wealth among the chronologically old, who as a group already are comparatively well-off, requires an equal deprivation among the young and the poorer old. This implies a loss of purchasing power among most of the population, which could partially offset the forces promoting economic growth. Nonetheless, the overall economic effect of life extension will be positive.

- Per capita personal income increased 1.4 percent annually from 1973 to 1983 and 1.5 percent annually between 1980 and 1991. This rise will average 1.45 percent annually through the turn of the century.

- Part of society's affluence rests on the use or overuse of credit cards. Extension of excessive credit could result in government-imposed limitations, especially on credit rates.

- The intolerably high interest rates of the 1970s have led the Federal Reserve Board to "manage" interest rates since 1981. As a result, interest rates have held for several years near the bottom of their twenty-year range. Throughout the early twenty-first century, they are unlikely to regain the heights they attained in the 1970s.

- FRB monetary policies instituted by John Volker and continued by Alan Greenspan will continue to keep interest and inflation rates in check. Housing starts will continue to grow, and building of all kinds will expand. The leading indicator in this area is building permits, which also display a continuing uptrend in the United States. This uptrend will remain particularly strong in the more distant suburbs.
- American exports should continue strong, as the U.S. dollar will remain relatively weak compared with its previous record against other currencies. Thus, the balance-of-trade deficit should hold fairly stable.
- Automobiles sales will slow as the useful life of cars stretches from its current average of about nine years to a bit more than two decades. American cars should retain much of the market share they once lost, and recently have begun to recover, because the mean time between failure is virtually the same for all cars now being sold. Whether cars are American, German, or Japanese, the same robots are building them. The 20-something Generation X will continue to fire the market for sport utility vehicles. Between 2005 and 2010, when consumers begin to recognize that they no longer face a gradual decline into "old age," a burst of general euphoria may spur sales of high-end automobiles and other luxury items. As personal incomes begin to decline, consumers will retrench, and sales of big-ticket items will decline.

2. The growth of the information industries is creating a knowledge-dependent society.

- Service workers will make up 88 percent of the U.S. labor force by 2000. Half of them will be involved in collecting, analyzing, synthesizing, structuring, storing, or retrieving information.
- By 2005, 83 percent of all management personnel will be knowledge workers.
- Functions such as the analysis and synthesis of information usually benefit from years of experience. Life-extended

workers will be particularly desirable for positions emphasizing these skills.

- By 2005, half of all knowledge workers (22 percent of the labor force) will opt for "flextime, flexplace" arrangements, which allow them to work at home, communicating with the office via computer terminals.
- Life extension will bring new growth to the service sector. Most of the additional jobs will appear in the hospitality and leisure industries, business and financial services, and home-oriented convenience services for the well-to-do.
- The computer industry will continue to offer vast opportunities for creative entrepreneurs. Though hardware remains promising, software developers will reap the greatest rewards. However, profits in the software industry will be divided between many more companies and people.
- Expert systems will issue reports and recommend actions based on data gathered electronically, without human intervention. By 2005, they will become an important tool in the health-care industry, which will use them both to replace human doctors for run-of-the-clinic illnesses and to ensure that patients receive the least expensive treatment consistent with effective care.
- Investment in expert systems and related technologies has grown from $35 million in 1986 to well over $1 billion. What some of these applications do can be startling. One Nebraska newspaper reportedly now uses a computer program to write at least some of its sports stories; plug in a few basic facts, and the software can churn out a thrilling report of a game. The pace of both development and investment will accelerate as far into the future as we can discern. In the process, it will displace many human workers.
- Industries that benefit from expert systems include insurance, investments and banking, manufacturing and process control, equipment diagnosis, and quality control.
- By 2005, nearly all college textbooks and many high school and junior high books will come with CD-ROMs to aid in learning.

- Computers will provide access to the card catalogs of all the libraries in the world by the late 1990s. It will be possible to call up on a PC screen millions of volumes from distant libraries. Videodiscs enhance books by providing pictures, sound, film clips, and flexible indexing and search utilities.
- Encyclopedia works, large reference volumes, and heavily illustrated manuals already are cheaper to produce and sell as CD-ROMs than in print form.

3. Great poverty and great wealth are becoming even less common in the United States, producing an increasingly uniform middle-class society. However, this trend will survive only until effective life-extending treatments begin to change the nation's demographic picture and the distribution of wealth. This alteration probably will become visible around 2015.

- The middle three-fifths of families have received 52 to 54 percent of money income since 1950. This proportion will grow slightly in the coming years.
- The number of households with annual incomes over $75,000 (in 1990 dollars) rose from 5.6 percent in 1970 to 9.7 percent in 1990, the most recent general census; those with incomes under $10,000 declined from 15.6 percent in 1970 to 14.9 percent in 1990.
- Among families, the trend is similar, but not identical. The number with annual incomes over $75,000 (in 1990 dollars) grew from 6.5 percent in 1970 to 12.3 percent in 1990. However, the fraction with incomes under $10,000 also increased, from 8.7 percent in 1970 to 9.4 percent in 1990.
- Statistics overstate the number of very poor in the United States, because they omit income equivalents such as food stamps, housing allowances, and free medical care, which improve the recipient's standard of living much as a paycheck would. When these are included, the poverty rate falls sharply. Official figures show that 10.5 percent have incomes under $10,000 per year. The effective figure, taking income supplements into account, is closer to 6 to 7 percent.

- However, there is a significant imbalance between the ends of the income scale. The upper 1 percent of American earners received 10 percent of the nation's income as of 1995. So did the bottom 19 percent.
- The fraction of the nation's wealth owned by the very rich is even more disproportionately large. Less than 2 percent of the nation's households own some 40 percent of its wealth. This imbalance will grow worse, as the rich will make up a smaller percentage of the population yet will continue to own a large and growing portion of its wealth.
- Higher taxes for people whose income is over $180,000 per family will tend to slow the growth of the number of very wealthy in our society.
- But recent welfare "reforms" in the United States have dramatically reduced the benefit of income supplements. As a result, the number of genuinely poor people in the United States may begin to rise again in the first decade of the new century.
- Even more important, as part of federal budget balancing, small businesses structured as proprietorships or partnerships or as Subchapter S corporations will be taxed at the same rate as individuals. This will reduce job growth in the economic sector where most new jobs have previously appeared.
- To offset that, and to restore job growth, the Clinton administration has agreed to reduce the tax on capital gains.
- At the same time, the burden for poorer taxpayers has eased slightly.
- Some of the reforms now contemplated for Social Security eventually will pass, including means testing and taxation of benefits. Yet even these changes will be much too conservative for a life-extended nation. Today's recipients will live longer than planners forecast, and life-extended Boomers can expect several more decades of retirement than anyone ever imagined. Thus, revenues needed will be much higher than anticipated. This will place an undue burden on people of working age. Taxes on nearly everyone with an income

will be raised to help pay for the benefits now committed to retirees.

- By dramatically reducing the incidence of cancer, heart disease, and the many other ills of old age, life extension should cut our national health-care bill by at least 50 percent. Money saved from Medicare should partially make up for the higher cost of Social Security. This change may even make universal health insurance affordable.

4. Rural land is being colonized by suburbs and cities. Land in farms has decreased steadily since 1959. The rate of decline was 1 percent per year from 1975 to 1985 and slowed to 0.5 percent per year between 1985 and 1991. Between 1991 and 1996, it has risen to 0.9 percent.

- Suburbs are developing more rapidly than cities, largely because land there is cheaper, road systems are better, and modern telecommunications provide easy access. (For example, Gateway Computer, one of the largest makers of personal computers in the United States, does all its business from rural North Dakota.) Three-fourths of the U.S. population live in cities, including their nearest suburbs, and only one-fourth in rural areas.
- Suburbia is being urbanized, as satellite cities grow outside the major metropolitan areas. Construction of office parks, shopping centers, and entertainment districts is creating suburban "downtowns."
- Population is expanding from the suburbs into outlying towns and rural areas, creating a new "penturbia."
- "Superburbs" will connect cities in the South and West, where most of the population growth over the next decade is expected to occur.
- Serious overcrowding in the retirement communities of the Sun Belt could keep affluent oldsters in penturbia. Some may retire to major cities, where they can enjoy cultural events and similar attractions. Many others will simply continue their careers and live wherever work takes them. In the most

desirable regions, competition from a larger population could raise land values.

5.   Growing acceptance of cultural diversity is combining with the unifying effect of mass media to promote the growth of a truly integrated national society. However, this is subject to change.

- Our beliefs and values are shaped by what we see and hear. Throughout the United States, people see the same movies and TV programs.
- Schools across the country teach essentially the same attitudes.
- Information technologies promote long-distance communication as people hook up with the same commercial databases and computer networks, and above all with the Internet. Interactive cable television will accelerate this process.
- New modes of transportation, the adoption of automated traffic-management systems and other highway technologies (especially on the Interstate system), more and better accommodations (thanks to the growth of the hospitality industry), more leisure time, and greater affluence will allow more frequent travel. Common-carrier passenger miles grew by 4 percent per year from 1982 to 1985 and by 3.7 percent from 1985 to 1990, and will continue to grow at roughly 3.9 percent through the beginning of the next century. This will produce a greater interplay of ideas, information, and concerns.
- Regional differences, attitudes, incomes, and lifestyles are blurring as people move from one region to another.
- Intermarriage also continues to mix cultures geographically, ethnically, socially, and economically.
- Minorities will exert more influence over the national agenda as the number of blacks, Hispanics, and Asians increases from 17 percent of the population in 1990 to 33 percent by 2000.
- By 2015, life extension may begin to reverse this growing co-

hesion by sharpening the competition for resources among age and economic groups. Caucasians will dominate the oldest and most influential generation, while Hispanics and African Americans will make up much more of the younger age groups. As older, primarily Caucasian investors absorb still more of the nation's wealth, younger minority workers will blame them for their own relative discomfort. Less-well-to-do retirees who are forced back into the job market in turn may seek scapegoats for their problems. If so, they will find them among minorities and immigrants.

6. The permanent military establishment continues to shrink in numbers.

- More and better-trained reserve and National Guard units will reduce the need for permanent, professional troops.
- Smart weapons will tend to reduce the need for military personnel.
- Orders for new and replacement weapons are being cut back.
- The military is consolidating and eliminating bases.
- By 2005, young men, and probably women, can expect to spend two years in compulsory national service. They will have three options: military service, VISTA/Americorps-type work with poor and disabled, or duty with the Peace Corps.
- By 2015, these programs may become the only realistic hope of secure, if not particularly well paid, employment left to young people who lack a sound education in a marketable field. Bottom-rung jobs in the service industries will be their only other opportunity.

7. Americans grow increasingly mobile in key areas: personal life, location, occupations, jobs.

- In the five years from 1980 to 1985, 41.7 percent of the U.S. population moved. From 1987 to 1988, the number was 17.6 percent of the population annually; since then it has been about 17 percent per year, or one-third of the population every two years. We expect Americans to remain highly mobile throughout the foreseeable future.

- Dual-career families, with partners sometimes working in different cities, require greater personal mobility. One or both partners may commute long distances to remain in their established home, the family may move to some intermediate location, or one partner may change jobs to be nearer the other's place of business.
- Modular housing and mobile homes made largely of plastic will reach the market between 2005 and 2015, allowing people to move more frequently and easily. Owners will simply pack up their houses and ship them to the new locale.
- Transportation systems are available and accessible to all. High-speed rail systems similar to Japan's "bullet trains" and the French TGV system will allow commutes of up to 500 miles. By 2005, such systems should be in operation between Boston and Washington, D.C., with a stop in New York; between Los Angeles and Reno; and between Chicago and several outlying cities.
- The Global Positioning System, a constellation of navigation satellites lofted by the U.S. military, now can pinpoint the location of a ship, an airplane, or even a package to within a few feet.
- Global satellite communication will be available by 2000. A person equipped with a wireless telephone or modem will be able to speak to anyone, send a fax, or tie into computers anywhere in the world, twenty-four hours a day.
- Occupational mobility grows as people increasingly retrain for new careers.
- The new information-based model for the organization—a nonhierarchical, organic system able to respond quickly to environmental changes—fosters greater occupational flexibility and automony.
- Job mobility—the freedom to change location or firm while doing the same work—is spreading. People soon will expect to switch jobs four to five times during a career, and to change entire careers every decade.

- Jobs will continue their migration to Sun Belt states, right-to-work states, and seaboard states.

8. International affairs and national security are becoming major factors within society.

- More international travel for business and pleasure brings greater exposure to other societies, and to foreign political turmoil.
- International student exchange programs are proliferating.
- Observation/verification activity between the East and West has grown since the end of the Cold War.
- So have East-West cultural exchanges.
- Television and radio satellite hookups are promoting the cross-pollination of diverse cultures. The Internet already is hastening this process.
- Regional political and economic arrangements such as the European Community, the Organization of American States, the North American Free Trade Agreement, and the nascent Pacific/Indian Ocean alliance are playing a larger role in world political and economic affairs.
- The international treaty signed at Rio in 1995 was only the first step toward environmental cooperation on a global scale.
- The West and the United States are pumping large amounts of money into the former Eastern Bloc countries to aid their economies in the transition from communism and socialism to democracy.
- This global integration means that people in the less developed countries will immediately learn of life-extending therapies. Because life extension appears not to require costly technologies or expensive drugs, it will be available to the Third World unless political restrictions intervene. Populations in Africa, Asia, and Latin America could grow even faster and sink even farther into poverty.
- Tensions between the rich and poor lands could grow much worse.

- The idea that the rich lands of the West have found a way to extend what others sometimes perceive to be lives of luxury and decadence could further anger the educated, but often poor and hopeless, young people of the Third World, who already provide the manpower for many terrorist organizations. This may depend on the reactions of fundamentalist religious leaders, who could well view life extension as blasphemously contravening the will of God.

THE TECHNOLOGY TRENDS

9. Technology increasingly dominates both the economy and society.

- In all fields, the previous state of the art is being replaced by new high-tech developments ever faster. (See Trend 16.)
- Technological advances such as more powerful personal computers, robotics, and CAD/CAM directly affect the way people live and work.
- Mundane commercial and service jobs, environmentally dangerous jobs, and assembly and repair of space-station components in orbit increasingly will be done by robots. Personal robots will appear in the home by 2005.
- Computers are fast becoming part of our environment, rather than just tools we use for specific tasks. With wireless modems, portable computers give us access to networked data wherever we go.
- Satellite-based telephone systems and Internet connections and other wireless links will simplify relocation of personnel, minimize delays in accomplishing new installations, and let terminals travel with the user instead of forcing the user to seek out the terminal.
- By 2001, artificial intelligence and virtual reality will help most companies and government agencies to assimilate data and solve problems beyond the range of today's computers. AI's uses include robotics, machine vision, voice recognition,

speech synthesis, electronic data processing, health and human services, administration, and airline pilot assistance.

- By 2001, expert systems will permeate manufacturing, energy prospecting, automotive diagnostics, medicine, insurance underwriting, and law enforcement.
- Superconductors operating at room temperature will be in commercial use by 2015. Products will include supercomputers the size of three-pound coffee cans, electric motors 75 percent smaller and lighter than those today, practical hydrogen-fusion power plants, electrical storage facilities with no heat loss, and noninvasive analyzers that can chart the interaction of brain cells.
- The engineering, technology, and health industries will all grow rapidly, and many new biotechnology jobs will open up.
- The availability of a pool of experienced, relatively well-educated workers in what once would have been the retirement age could well supply both R&D and management personnel to speed the adoption of new technologies. However, older workers will have to strive especially hard to keep their professional knowledge and cultural attitudes up to date.

10. Technological advances in transportation will dispel the threat of national gridlock in the air and on land. This will further promote the mobility foretold by Trend 8.

- By 2005 or so, high-speed trains will begin to replace the spokes of the airline industry's existing hub-and-spoke system for journeys of 100 to 150 miles.
- By 2010, New York, Tokyo, and Frankfurt will emerge as transfer points for passengers of high-speed supersonic planes.
- The average life of a car in the United States soon will be twenty-two years. For the Volvo, it is already nearing twenty years.
- Advances in automobile technology are rapidly giving us the "smart car." Standard features soon will include equipment

available now only as costly options—antilock brakes, active suspension, and global positioning receivers that make it all but impossible to get lost—and gadgets still under development: road-condition sensors, computer-orchestrated fuel-injection systems, continuously variable transmission, automated traffic-management systems, and many other innovations. These all will be in common use by 2010.

- Between 2005 and 2010, fuel-efficient hybrid gas-electric cars will begin to win market share from traditional gas guzzlers.
- The United States will lag in adopting new highway technology. Though systems that allow traffic lights and the roadbed itself to interact with cars are already available, it will not be until at least 2005 that Washington begins to install them in the most heavily used roadways throughout the country.
- To reduce the number and severity of traffic accidents, trucks will be exiled to car-free lanes, and the separation will be enforced.
- Airline crashes will decline, and will involve fewer fatalities, thanks to such technical advances as safer seat design, flash-resistant fuels, and the use of satellites for navigation and communication in transoceanic flights.

11. The national economy is growing more integrated at both the wholesale and retail levels, and even in government-spending priorities.

- Rather than paying salaries and benefits for activities that do not contribute directly to their bottom line, companies are farming out secondary functions to suppliers, service firms, and consultants, which often are located in other regions of the country.
- This "outsourcing" is helping to trim payrolls and is making it ever less likely that today's workers will enjoy a traditional retirement. At the same time, it will give tomorrow's active aged the chance to remain productive as consultants and part-time workers.
- New industrial standards—for building materials, fasteners,

even factory machines—allow both civilian and government buyers to order from almost any supplier, rather than only from those with whom they have established relationships. The proliferation of standards is one of the most important industrial trends now operating.

- To aid in "just-in-time" purchasing, many suppliers are giving customers direct online access to their computerized ordering and inventory systems. Increasingly often, the order goes directly from the customer to the shop floor, and even into the supplier's automated production equipment. Many manufacturers will no longer deal with suppliers who cannot provide this access, and the number grows daily.

- Computer networks and cable-TV home-shopping channels are bringing retailers and manufacturers closer to distant customers, who have been out of reach until now.

- At the federal level, defense and social programs are no longer effectively separated. From now on, they will compete for funding; so will health and education, infrastructure, and the environment.

- New procurement regulations and standards also promise to open the government market to suppliers who previously found the bidding process too difficult, costly, or just confusing.

12. The national economy is becoming integrated with the international economy.

- Imports continue to increase, international capital markets are merging, and buying patterns around the world coalesce. All these factors promote the interdependence of business and government decisions worldwide.

- Foreigners own $1.5 trillion in U.S. assets, one-fourth more than the value of assets the United States owns abroad.

- Some 42 percent of the parts used in American manufacturing originate overseas. By the turn of the century, over half the parts in any manufactured good will come from a foreign country.

- This trend is not limited to the United States. Japan must sell internationally to offset the cost of importing energy and scarce resources.
- National self-interest will continue to promote the growth of international trade cooperation. Both developing and developed countries will focus less on dominating economic competitors and instead will put their efforts into liberalizing trade cooperation.
- ISO standards are being adopted throughout the world, so that every country can supply parts and machinery for every other, with an effective guarantee of compatibility and quality.
- America's extended-agers will be competing for their living not only with younger Americans and new immigrants, but with low-income workers throughout the world. Those who cannot support themselves with capital or with unique skills will fall to the lower segments of the economy.
- In short, they face exactly the same economic future we all do, but for a lot longer than they once expected.

13. The international economy will gain importance throughout the early twenty-first century.

- Witness the interactions among the world's stock exchanges. A sharp drop in, say, Tokyo follows the sun to exchanges in Hong Kong, Paris, London, and eventually New York.
- Consumers around the world are demanding greater quality in products and services.
- Deregulation also is spreading around the world.
- Privatization is a growing trend. Governments around the world are selling off public services and returning nationalized industries to private hands.
- In the United States, this could mean an end to the U.S. Postal Service's monopoly on regular mail service.
- Abroad, it will cause a transition from federal to private ownership of airlines, railroads, petrochemicals, water, and electricity.

14. Research and development plays a growing role in the economy.

   - R&D outlays as a percentage of GNP have varied narrowly (from 2.1 to 2.8 percent) since 1960. They rose steadily in the decade after 1978, then stabilized in 1988. Future increases will pace the growth of the GNP.
   - R&D outlays are growing most rapidly in the electronics, aerospace, pharmaceuticals, and chemical industries. One result of this can be seen in the prosperity of the NASDAQ stock market, which emphasizes research-oriented industries.
   - Any dramatic reduction in the ills of old age should free research funds for other purposes, one of which almost surely will be the further prolongation of healthy life. Most of the markets for pharmaceuticals will decline as the ills of senescence—heart disease, cancer, arthritis, diabetes, and so on—begin to disappear along with the conditions that once made us vulnerable to them.
   - However, antidepressants and other drugs aimed at mental health could be in for a boom as people struggle to redefine their lives in a world of changing values no longer dictated by the inevitability of death.

15. The pace of technological change accelerates with each new generation of discoveries and applications.

   - The design and marketing cycle—idea, invention, innovation, imitation—is shrinking steadily. Successful products must be marketed quickly, before the competition can copy them. As late as the 1940s, the product cycle stretched to thirty or forty years. Today it seldom lasts thirty or forty weeks.
   - Industry will adopt new production technologies as rapidly as they can be developed.
   - Computer-aided design in the automobile and other industries shortens the lag time between idea and finished design.

- All the technological knowledge we work with today will represent only 1 percent of the knowledge that will be available in 2050.
- This may mean that extended-age workers will be at a relative disadvantage, because the technological age demands extreme flexibility and fast turnaround. It depends on how much we ossify as a result of time and habit, rather than from biological decay. Future generations may well adopt attitudes, or develop psychological therapies, that better fit them to a culture of rapid, permanent change. The pioneers of extended aging could find it more difficult to remain productive.

16. Mass telecommunications and printing are continuing to bind the country, and the world.

- Telecommunications removes geographic barriers. India, Pakistan, and parts of the Caribbean have built thriving industries keyboarding computer data for the United States and Europe. In these regions, it costs only $.50 per hour to have two people type data into a computer and reconcile their mistakes. Including two-way satellite transmission to and from the United States, the total cost is roughly $1.50. In the United States, it costs $5 per hour to have one person enter data.
- The "integrated information appliance" will combine a computer, a fax, a picture phone, and a duplicator in one unit for less than $2,500 (in 1995 dollars) by the year 2002. The picture will appear on a flat screen of twenty inches by thirty inches. By 2005 or so, such units will include real-time voice translation, so that conversations originating in any of seven or eight common languages can be heard in any of the others.
- Both the *Wall Street Journal* and *USA Today,* relying on satellite communications, are printed simultaneously at multiple sites every day.
- Company-owned and industry-wide television networks are

bringing programming to thousands of locations. Business TV is becoming big business.

- Today, 72 percent of households with televisions have cable TV. The proportion will reach 87 percent soon after the turn of the century.
- General-interest magazines in the year 2005 will be published on CD-ROMs that allow the "reader" to interact, play with, and manipulate the information on a PC.
- Mass media will be more personalized as consumers use pay-for-view television to select movies and entertainment.
- Computer systems will create personalized newspapers by logging onto news-service databases at night, selecting stories and pictures and laying them out, setting the headlines in sizes that reflect their importance to the reader.
- The Internet, corporate intranets, wireless modems, and satellite communications systems, all interlinked in novel ways, are making possible a host of new data and communications services formerly undreamed of. By 2005, these services will be rapidly changing the way we work and live.
- This will require adoption of technically sound standards for the interfaces between users and the network, as well as among network elements.
- The nearly unlimited bandwidth of fiber optics, coupled with evolving network standards and the ability to use software-defined networks, will create new net topologies. Improved line-width lasers or dispersion-shifted fibers, multi-gigabit systems, coherent detection systems, LEDs for single-mode fibers, and integrated optical circuits will be in widespread use.

17. In the industrialized lands, our lives are about to be extended by decades.

- Supplements of melatonin, a harmless natural hormone whose levels decline as we grow older, keep laboratory animals healthy, vigorous, and young-looking to an age equivalent to 115 human years. There is no guarantee that melatonin itself will work similar wonders for people. However, this breakthrough in our understanding of the aging process clearly opens the way to practical age-preventing therapies. The first should be available within the next fifteen years—assuming that it has not arrived already.

- This first life extension will give researchers time to seek out further breakthroughs. Well before the Baby Boom generation reaches its extended life span, the next advance in anti-aging treatment should further set back our personal expiration dates, perhaps indefinitely.

18. Many other important medical advances will continue to appear almost daily. (See also Trends 51 and 52.)

- The discovery that a hormone called human chorionic gonadotropin, or hCG, appears in all cancer cells tested thus far, and (among adults) only in cancer cells, seems to promise the development of a generalized "cure for cancer." If early tests pan out, by 2010, and possibly sooner, tumors will be treated routinely and successfully with simple injections in the family doctor's office.

- Because of these and other advances, the need for hospital and hospice care will plummet. Save where surgery is required, most patients will be treated at home by nurse practitioners, technicians, and other nonphysician providers. When, eventually, we come to the end of our life-extended days, any final illness is likely to be brief and relatively gentle. At worst, it will require a short period of hospice care, but not the kind of protracted hospital stay that many of us have come to fear.

- Genetic engineering already does more than $100 billion worth of business, and there is much more to come. Thanks in large part to the Human Genome Project, which is running well ahead of schedule, scientists soon will know the structure and function of all the 50,000 or so genes that go to make up a human being. Already, this research has yielded possible cures for hemophilia, cystic fibrosis, familial hyper-cholesterolemia, a variety of cancers, and AIDS. At the same time, scientists are producing new, more nutritious crops that can grow in harsh climates, bacteria capable of making industrially important chemicals, and many other products. The flood of new medical advances and industrial products from genetic engineering will continue for at least the next twenty-five years.

- Though not so versatile, cloning technology offers many other new developments, from more productive farm animals to grow-your-own artificial organs. Such theoretical possibilities as cloned people are unlikely to materialize, but less controversial applications should be in general use by 2010.
- Artificial blood will be on the market by 2000. By 2005, it could begin to replace the nation's blood banks.
- Memory-enhancing drugs should reach clinical use by 2005.
- Newborns will be artificially endowed with particular disease immunities.
- The ethical issues raised by technologies such as organ transplants, artificial organs, genetic engineering, cloning, and DNA mapping will cause a growing public debate. Among the key problems: surrogate motherhood, how to distribute medical resources equitably, when to terminate extraordinary life-support efforts, and whether fetal tissues should be transplanted to adults in order to combat disease. In the end, these debates will be resolved on the side of disease prevention. Therapies designed to correct genetic defects will be accepted. Elective procedures intended to change eye or skin color, or even for generally desirable goals, such as to improve intelligence or physical stamina, will be banned.
- New computer-based diagnostic tools will give doctors unprecedented images of soft and hard tissues inside the body, eliminating much exploratory surgery.
- "Magic bullet" drug-delivery systems will make it possible to direct enormous doses of medication exactly where they

are needed, sparing the rest of the body from possible side effects. This will improve therapeutic results in many conditions that require the use of powerful drugs.

- "Bloodless surgery" using advanced lasers will reduce patient trauma, shorten hospital stays, and help lower medical costs.
- Brain-cell and nerve-tissue transplants to aid victims of retardation, head trauma, and other neurological disorders will enter clinical use by 2005. So will heart repairs using muscles from other parts of the body. Transplanted animal organs will find their way into common use. Laboratory-grown bone, muscle, and blood cells also will be used in transplants.
- Pacemakers will contain built-in shockers (like the paddles in the emergency room), saving heart patients even before emergency medical personnel arrive.
- In the next ten years, we expect to see more and better bionic limbs and hearts, drugs that prevent disease rather than merely treating symptoms, and body monitors that warn of impending trouble.
- By the year 2000, some 85 percent of doctors will be salaried and working for health maintenance organizations and other prepaid medical plans.
- Generic drugs will account for well over half of prescriptions by 2000. By 2005, many of them will be purchased over the Internet, just as they have been bought by mail order since the 1970s.
- As life-extending technologies give the elderly a level of health and vitality once reserved for much younger people, we will become much less susceptible to the diseases of old age. Thus, we will need fewer doctors, nurses, and facilities to deal with victims of cancer, heart disease, diabetes, and other age-related disorders.
- Genetic disorders, trauma, viral diseases, Third World bacterial and parasitic infections, and so on will become comparatively more significant.

- We can expect a major push against Alzheimer's disease, if anti-aging therapies fail to prevent this disorder.
- It is at least possible that some entirely new diseases will appear, or rare ones become more common, because we no longer die before they have time to manifest themselves. This does not seem likely, as vulnerability to disease is far more characteristic of old age than of youth. No such phenomenon is seen in life-extended animals.
- Far more mental-health care and counseling will be required as people who grew up in a world of limited life span must adapt to the prospect of living decades longer than they expected. The psychological implications of extended life are likely to be complicated. Some may find the prospect liberating, others frightening.

EDUCATIONAL TRENDS

19. Education and training are expanding throughout society.

- President Clinton and his administration advocate greater federal spending both for education and training. We expect the money to be found.
- Needed: an annual $10 billion increase in federal spending for programs such as Head Start, federal aid for disadvantaged children, the Job Corps, and the Job Training Partnership Act.
- The half-life of an engineer's knowledge today is only five years; in ten years, 90 percent of what an engineer knows will be available on the computer.
- Eighty-five percent of the information in National Institutes of Health computers is upgraded in five years.
- Rapid changes in the job market and work-related technologies will necessitate increased training for virtually every American worker.
- Automation, international competition, and other funda-

mental changes in the economy are destroying the few remaining well-paid jobs that do not require advanced training.

- In the next ten years, close to 10 million jobs will open up for professionals, executives, and technicians in the highly skilled service occupations. However, many of these positions may be for part-time workers.

- A substantial portion of the labor force will be in job-retraining programs at any moment. Much of this will be carried out by current employers, who have come to view employee training as a good investment. Major corporations report that they earn between $20 and $30 for every dollar they put into employee training.

- Schools will train both children and adults around the clock. The academic day will stretch to seven hours for children; adults will work a thirty-two-hour week and prepare for their next job in the remaining time.

- State, local, and private agencies will play a greater role in training by offering more internships, apprenticeships, pre-employment training, and adult education.

- Professional alliances between high school and college faculties will spread rapidly. One popular option will be "2+2+2 programs" involving high schools, two-year colleges, and four-year colleges.

- We already are seeing a trend toward more adult education. One reason is the necessity to train for new careers as old ones are displaced or Boomers grow bored with them. The other is the need of healthy, energetic people to keep active during retirement. Life extension will amplify both these forces, resulting in even greater demand for midlife and later-life schooling.

20. New technologies will greatly ease this process.

- Job-simulation stations—modules that combine computers, CD-ROMs, and instrumentation to duplicate job skills and work environments—will be used in training.

- Telecommunications coursework with other, often far-distant, school districts will open up new vistas in education.
- Education is becoming more individualized, as interactive computer/CD-ROM systems and other new media permit students to learn according to their needs and abilities.
- Personal computers with ultrahigh-resolution screens, 3-D graphics, high-level interactivity, artificial intelligence, and virtual reality will enhance gaming and simulations used in education and training.

21. Business is taking on a greater role in training and education.

- More companies will participate in school, job-training, and community-resource programs.
- Corporations now invest some $42 billion per year in employee education and retraining. Some 68 percent of employers now say they would prefer to hire workers with job training instead of college graduates.
- Automation and computers replace many low-literacy jobs with fewer jobs that require a high degree of literacy. Businesses will have to give their workers continuous training to keep up with these growing demands.
- Most new jobs are generated by small businesses, which cannot afford to pay for training. Half of all funding for formal training comes from the 200 to 300 largest companies in business and industry. Of the $42 billion spent on employee training each year, 95 percent is spent by companies with over 300 workers.
- Business education and job training will become more important for older adults who remain in the workforce. Older workers may well be seen as more desirable, because they already have the training and experience that younger workers need. This is especially likely if senior executives (in both senses) hang on to their positions into what formerly were the retirement years; they are likely to be most comfortable with colleagues of their own age group.

22. Education costs will continue to rise.

   - Heavy pressure to control costs will emerge.
   - Costs may reach the point where they threaten to reduce the pool of college graduates over the next decade. (See Trend 49.)
   - Two-year colleges and associate degrees will gain popularity, because they are more affordable than four-year programs.
   - Five-year co-op college programs also will increase dramatically in the rest of the decade.
   - Loans rather than grants will provide most student financial aid.

23. Educational reforms are spreading through the United States.

   - The information economy requires skilled workers; this necessitates more effective schooling.
   - Lackluster performance of American students on standardized tests also will prompt inevitable reforms.
   - Science and engineering schools will actively recruit more students.
   - Policy changes to ease the burden on the U.S. school system may include lengthening the school year to 210 seven-hour days and cutting class size from an average of 17.8 students to ten.

24. Educational institutions will pay more attention to the outcomes and effectiveness of their programs.

   - In part, this will be forced on them by growing demand from the public and from state legislatures.
   - Faculty will (often reluctantly) support efforts to assess their classroom performance and effectiveness.
   - Academic departments will also support assessment of their academic programs' results and effectiveness.

- More states will adopt the national education goals to assess their school performance.

25. Improved pedagogy—the science of learning—will revolutionize learning.

- Institutions will adapt their educational situations to fit our growing knowledge about individual cognition.
- The learning environment will not be as important in future, because individuals will learn more on their own, the "places" of learning will be more dispersed, and the age at which things are learned will depend on individual ability rather than tradition.
- Unconventional learning techniques will help boost memory skills in the future.
- Computer-supported approaches to learning will improve educational techniques and make it possible to learn more in a given period.
- The ultimate consequence may be a one-sixth reduction in learning time overall.
- Despite the new technologies and approaches to education, many students will still suffer from learning deficiencies.
- Alternative testing approaches will be widely adopted for feedback on course effectiveness.
- Because our learning styles change as we grow older, all of these new teaching methods may have to be adapted to fit the demands of extended life.

26. Universities will stress development of the whole student, redesigning the total university environment to promote that development.

- Faculty will receive greater support from the administration for class-related activities.
- Individual students will receive more support from faculty and advisers in their academic programs and career paths.

27. Institutions of higher education are shrinking.

  - By 2001 there will not be enough adolescents to sustain the current number of colleges and universities. Colleges will close their doors, merge with other schools in federations, reduce faculty size and class offerings, and seek more adult students.
  - Private commercial ventures will establish themselves as the proprietors of large electronic databases, eventually replacing the university library.
  - Students will adopt the scholarship mode of learning—learning by consulting books, journals, and primary resources—as professors and Ph.D. candidates do today.
  - College and university instructors will find employment at secondary schools, in business-based education programs, and in producing educational electronic software.
  - More and more businesses will conduct research.

TRENDS IN LABOR FORCE AND WORK

28. Specialization is spreading throughout industry and the professions.

  - For doctors, lawyers, engineers, and other professionals, the size of the body of knowledge required to excel in a particular area precludes excellence across all areas.
  - The same principle applies to artisans. Witness the rise of post-and-beam home builders, old-house restorers, automobile electronics technicians, and mechanics trained to work on only one brand of car.
  - The information-based organization is dependent upon its teams of task-focused specialists.
  - Globalization of the economy calls for the more independent specialists. For hundreds of tasks, corporations will turn to consultants and independent contractors who specialize

more and more narrowly as markets globalize and technologies differentiate.

29. Services are the fastest-growing sector of the American economy.

- The service sector employed 70 percent by 1990 and soon will grow to nearly 90 percent. The Bureau of Labor Statistics projects a 1.6 percent annual growth for the period 1990 to 2005.
- Service jobs have replaced many of the well-paid jobs lost in manufacturing, transportation, and agriculture. These new jobs, often part-time, pay half the wages of manufacturing jobs.
- Only 1 million new jobs will appear in the less skilled and laborer categories in the next decade.

30. The agricultural and manufacturing sectors continue to shrink.

- Agriculture and mining employ 0.4 percent less of the American labor force each year. We expect this rate of decline to persist through at least 2005.
- There will be 1.25 million farmers in the United States in 2000; this is 900,000 less than in 1990. However, farm production will triple in that period.
- By 2001, manufacturing will employ only 9.7 percent of the labor force, down from 18 percent in 1987. However, productivity will rise 500 percent in industries that become more automated, add robotics, and remain flexible in their production. By comparison, construction employment will remain relatively stable, thanks to new building required by a prosperous economy.
- The evolution of new materials and production technology—CAD, CAM, robotics, and automation—will eliminate the few unskilled and semiskilled jobs that still survive in manufacturing.

31. The information industries are growing rapidly, and creating an information society in the process. (This is an outgrowth of Trend 2.)

- By the year 2000, we predict that 88 percent of the labor force will work in the service sector. Of that 88 percent, half will be working in the information industry, and one-fourth will be working at home.
- Information is the primary commodity in more and more industries today.
- Computer competence will approach 100 percent in U.S. urban areas by the year 2005.
- Eighty percent of U.S. homes will have computers in 2005, compared to 35 percent now. More than three-fourths will be equipped to permit communication with the Internet and commercial network services. Already, some 23 percent of adults in the United States and Canada use the Internet. This will grow to more than 50 percent by 2005.
- Computers in the home will provide vast new powers over information and services. They will revolutionize education, work, health care, shopping, banking and finance, reservations, and many other fields.
- The amount of information accessible through home computers (from telephone links and from extremely-high-capacity disks) will be so vast that we will require artificially intelligent electronic assistants to sort through it.
- Interactive cable television will combine with the Internet to create a need for electronic newspapers, electronic shopping, and electronic banking at home.
- Personal computers will be used to vote, file income tax returns, apply for auto license plates, and take college entrance exams and professional accreditation tests.
- Five of the ten fastest growing careers between now and 2005 will be computer-related. Demand for programmers and systems analysts will grow by 70 percent.
- ISDN (Integrated Digital Services Network) and similar

technologies will cut the cost of data acquisition and transmission by eliminating modems and by allowing data to share telecommunication facilities with voice services.

- Sophisticated computer networks using shared expert systems will provide medical advice, warn of likely illnesses, execute financial transactions, select travel and entertainment options before reservation limits are exceeded, and assist in education, as well as offering basic voice and data communication. In short, telecommunications will become far more transparent as the metaphor bridging these discrete technologies becomes more natural.

- The major change that better communications links will deliver consumers is to give the small user access to databases such as real estate listings, store inventories, and financial information at much less cost and over much greater distances.

- Many states' economic development plans have tried to encourage high-tech industries, yet these industries account for only 4 to 5 percent of the new jobs created each year. Many more new jobs are opening up in businesses that use— rather than produce—computers and other high-technology equipment.

- The United States is home to more than 80 percent of the world's computer-related companies with annual sales of more than $1 billion each.

32. More women continue to enter the labor force.

- More work can be done at home, child-care facilities and services are improving, and many families require income from both spouses in order to survive.

- In 1970, 43 percent of women worked. Since then, the number has grown to 54.5 percent in 1985 and 57.3 percent in 1991. By 2005, 63 percent of working-age women will be in the labor force.

- Approximately 63 percent of new entrants into the labor force between 1985 and 2000 will be women. Between 1995

and 2000, 85 percent of all new hires will be either women or minorities.
- Expect new demands for child care as a result.
- Businesses will seek to fill labor shortages with stay-at-home mothers by offering child-care programs and job sharing.
- More flextime and flexplace opportunities will make it easier for women to enter the work force.
- In 75 percent of households, both partners will work full-time by the year 2005, up from 63 percent in 1992.

33. Women's salaries will slowly approach equality to men's.

- Women's salaries have grown from 61 percent of men's in 1960 to 64 percent in 1980, 68 percent in 1985, and 74 percent in 1991.
- This figure will be 83 percent or more by the year 2000.
- Historically, women's salaries in California and north of the Mason-Dixon Line have been higher (currently, 87 percent of men's); south of the line they have been lower (only 60 percent of men's).
- To the extent that experience translates into prestige and corporate value, older women should find it easier to reach upper-management positions. They will strengthen the nascent "old-girl" networks, which will help to raise the pay scale of women still climbing the corporate ladder.
- Older women may find it easier to become entrepreneurs as they gain confidence with experience and realize that they have extra decades of working life ahead of them.

34. More blacks and other minority groups are entering the labor force.

- Black workers made up only 9.2 percent of the civilian labor force in 1970 and 10.9 percent in 1980. By 1990, they had grown to 13.5 percent of the labor force. The figures will be 16.5 percent in 2000 and 17.8 percent in 2005.

- Hispanic workers formed 6.1 percent of the civilian labor force in 1980 and 9.8 percent in 1991. By 2000, they will make up 14.2 percent of the labor force; by 2005, 16.8 percent.
- Minorities constitute only 16 percent of the U.S. population, yet they account for 40 percent of AIDS cases.
- One out of six workers belonged to an ethnic minority in 1990. In the early twenty-first century, they will be one out of three.

- Minorities and the AARP will each have more political clout than the unions by the year 2000.

35. Workers are retiring later as life expectancy stretches.

- This trend has barely begun. By 2010, we expect the retirement age to be delayed well into the 70s—and even that may not be enough. A life-extended nation probably will have to delay the retirement age much longer, possibly by decades, beginning with the Baby Boom generation. Traditional retirement may not even be possible. Benefits may also continue their decline, and they will be given based on need, rather than as an entitlement.
- The usual retirement age will recede from age 65 to 67 to 70 even before the effects of life extension are felt.
- The military retirement age will be extended, and benefits will be converted to Social Security.
- The civil service retirement plan will also be converted to Social Security.
- People increasingly will work at one career, "retire" for a while (perhaps to travel) when they can afford it, return to school, begin another career, and so on in endless variations. True retirement, a permanent end to work, will be delayed until very late in an extended life.
- In the long run, it may prove impossible to maintain the tradition of retirement, save through personal savings and investment.

36. Unions are losing their power.

- Unions enrolled 28.9 percent of employed wage and salary workers in 1975, only 23.2 percent in 1980. By 1995, union membership had declined to less than 16.0 percent. By 2005, it will fall under 12 percent.
- The United Auto Workers projects less than 10 percent unionization by 2000.
- One reason is that jobs are moving constantly to no-union states or right-to-work states.
- Another is that the increased use of robots, CAD/CAM, and flexible manufacturing complexes can cut a company's workforce by up to one-third. The surviving workers tend to be technicians and other comparatively well-educated semi-professionals, who always have tended to resist union membership. The growing industrial use of artificial intelligence will further this trend.
- Ten or fifteen years into the next century, unions will compete with AARP to lead the battle for the rights of life-extended workers and for secure retirement benefits. They face an inherent conflict between the interests of workers in what once would have been the retirement years and those of younger members, who rightly see the elderly as having saddled them with the cost of whatever benefits other generations enjoy.

37. Pensions and pension funds continue to grow.

- Private pension and government retirement funds held only 4.2 percent of total institutional assets in 1970 and 5.8 percent fifteen years later, for an average annual increase of 2.8 percent. By 1991, they held 6.5 percent of institutional funds. This proportion may well slip, as workers opt to fund their own 401(k) retirement accounts and other private savings plans. This is by far the preferred option of the 20-something generation, which distrusts all institutions, and none more than Social Security.

- The presence of more people in the labor force for longer periods will add to pension-fund holdings during much of the next decade.
- However, as it becomes clear that life extension is a reality and the traditional retirement years will stretch on for extra decades, the solvency of pension funds will become a major issue of concern. In the end, they will have to be reorganized to provide not pensions but income supplements, so that the aged can work part-time, opening the way for younger workers. Full retirement will be possible only for the wealthy and for the rare individuals with medical problems that prevent them from working.
- They may be supplemented by targeted old-age funds intended to pay for living expenses and whatever medical care turns out to be necessary in the final years of a prolonged life.

38. Second and third careers are becoming common, as more people make midlife changes in occupation.

- People change careers every ten years, on average.
- A recent Louis Harris poll found that only 39 percent of workers say they intend to hold the same job five years from now; 31 percent say they plan to leave their current work; 29 percent do not know. (See Trend 39.)
- Boomers and their children will have not just two or three careers, but five, six, or even more, depending on how quickly science further extends the human span.

39. The work ethic is vanishing from American society.

- Tardiness is increasing.
- Sick-leave abuse is common.
- Job security and high pay are not the motivators they once were, because social mobility is high and people seek job fulfillment. Some 48 percent of those responding in a recent Louis Harris poll said they work because it "gives [them a] feeling of real accomplishment."

- Fifty-five percent of the top executives interviewed in the poll say that erosion of the work ethic will have a major negative effect on corporate performance in the future.
- In 1993, 60 percent of the college freshmen business students asked would have been willing to spend three years in jail, be considered a criminal, and have a jail record if their crime would net them $5 million.
- In a 1990 poll of American children, two-thirds said they would cheat to pass an important examination.
- In a 1991 survey of American adults, 90 percent admitted that they regularly lie.
- In a 1992 poll of the under-30 population, 38 percent said that being corrupt was "essential" in getting ahead.
- Yet, two-thirds of Americans would like to see an increase in the length of the work week rather than shorter hours.

40. Two-income couples are becoming the norm.

- They made up 38.4 percent of all married couples in 1980, 41.9 percent in 1985, and 46.9 percent in 1991. The figure will reach 75 percent by 2005. Life-extended couples will add to this trend as those in retirement age return to the workforce, either to augment pensions and Social Security, which will prove to be inadequate for the youthful elderly—if they can be sustained at all—or simply for something to do during all those extra years. Many of these couples will opt for part-time jobs rather than full-time employment, while others will start their own businesses.
- Look for families that usually have two incomes, but have frequent intervals in which one member takes a sabbatical or goes back to school to prepare for another career. As information technologies render former occupations obsolete, and extra decades of life render them intolerably boring, this will become the new norm.

41. Entry-level and low-wage workers will soon be in short supply.

- The declining birthrate in the 1960s and early 1970s means that fewer young people are entering the job market today. The number of jobs is increasing, creating entry-level labor shortages. This problem could be acute between 2000 and 2010, especially in the service sector.
- This may produce more entry-level job opportunities for high school graduates, as companies grow willing to train them on the job. However, these opportunities will not last much beyond 2015, when life-extended workers begin to compete for employment at all economic and skill levels.
- Colleges, business, and the military will vie for youths 16 to 24 years old, who will shrink from 20 percent of the labor force in 1985 to 16 percent in 2000.
- The educational level of military recruits will drop as competition from the private sector intensifies.
- Untapped pools of potential workers include the retarded and handicapped and stay-at-home mothers. Businesses will also increase automation and seek to attract more foreign workers.
- Hotels, restaurants, fast-food places, convenience stores, retailers, and businesses needing beginning computer and clerical skills will be especially hard hit by this labor shortage.
- This trend will ensure a growing demand for older workers, at least in the low-income industries.

MANAGEMENT TRENDS

42. More entrepreneurs start new businesses every year.

- For the newest generation of workers, those under 30, starting one's own company is the preferred manner of employment. Distrust of large companies, as of other institutions, is one reason. Another is the almost instinctive belief that jobs cannot provide a secure economic future in a time of rapid technological change.

- Since 1983, the number of new businesses started in the United States each year has never dipped below 600,000. In 1995, it reached a record 750,000, 4.5 times as many start-ups per capita as in 1950, when the economic boom after World War II was gathering momentum.
- The number of self-employed people in the United States increased from 7.5 percent in 1975 to more than 9 percent in 1995.
- More mid-career professionals will become entrepreneurs as they are squeezed out of the narrowing managerial pyramid in large companies. By 2001, only one person for every fifty will be promoted; in 1987, it was one person for every twenty.
- More women also are starting small businesses. Many are leaving traditional jobs to go home, open businesses, and have children.
- Ever since the 1970s, small businesses started by entrepreneurs have accounted for nearly all of the new jobs created. For much of this period, giant corporations have actually cut employment. In 1995, small, entrepreneurial businesses produced 1 million new full-time jobs vs. barely 100,000 produced by larger companies.
- By 2000, 80 percent of the labor force will be working for firms employing fewer than 200 people.
- This trend can only grow as the chronologically old but biologically young seek to build new careers on their own terms.

43. Information-based organizations are quickly displacing the old command-and-control model of management.

- Manual and clerical workers are being replaced with knowledge workers.
- Information technology is the driving force.

- Expect changes in management styles toward more participation by workers on a consultative basis.

44. The actual work will be done by task-focused teams of specialists.

   - The traditional department will assign the specialists, set the standards, and serve as the center for training.
   - Research, development, manufacturing, and marketing specialists will work together as a team on all stages of product development rather than keeping each stage separate and distinct.
   - Many of these teams will be coordinated by life-extended workers, who will combine the health and vigor of people in mid-career with a length of experience that virtually no one could have hoped to achieve before this. Who better to head a diversified team than someone who has spent four or five decades learning how projects are carried out and where they can go wrong?

45. The typical large business will be information-based, composed of specialists who rely on information from colleagues, customers, and headquarters to guide their actions.

   - Decision processes, management structure, and modes of work are being transformed as businesses take the first steps from using unprocessed data to using information—data that have been analyzed, synthesized, and organized in a useful way.
   - Computers have made possible this transformation of data to information.
   - Information-based organizations require more specialists, who will be found in operations, not at corporate headquarters.
   - Upper management will set clear performance expectations for the organization, its parts, and its specialists and supply

the feedback necessary to determine whether results have met expectations.

46. A typical large business in 2010 will have fewer than half the management levels of its counterpart today, and about one-third the number of managers.

- Middle management is fast disappearing as information flows directly up to higher management for analysis.
- Downsizing, restructuring, reorganization, outsourcing, and cutbacks of white-collar workers will continue through 2005.
- However, many companies are finding it necessary to bring back older workers, so as to preserve an effective corporate memory.
- Computers and information-management systems have stretched the manager's effective span of control from six to twenty-one subordinates; thus, fewer mid-level managers are needed. Top managers will have to be computer-literate to retain their jobs and must make sure they achieve that increased span of control.
- With major firms "trimming the fat," the pyramid will be flattened, with the specialists on the bottom.
- Opportunities for advancement will be few because they will come within the narrow specialty; bosses will refuse to die or to retire.
- Finding top managers will be extremely difficult until life extension provides an extra generation of experienced workers to fill these openings.
- Information-based organization will have to make a special effort to prepare professional specialists to become business executives and leaders.
- Thus, the values and compensation structure of business must change radically.

TRENDS IN VALUES AND CONCERNS

47. Societal values are changing rapidly.

- The "me" ethic of the 1980s has already been replaced by the "we" ethic, and a new "family" ethic has begun to appear.
- The open-endedness of extended life will force yet another rethinking of our values and priorities. Both self-reliance and group cooperation will be valued—self-reliance because we will no longer be able to fall back on Social Security, pensions, and other benefits; cooperation because group action often is the best way to optimize the use of scarce resources, such as retirement savings.
- Family issues will continue to dominate the society in the early twenty-first century: long-term health care, day care, early childhood education, antidrug campaigns, and the environment. Joining these familiar concerns will be all the questions raised by the generation of Baby Boom grandparents who are chronologically old but biologically young and economically unprepared for extra decades of life.
- Companies are now required to grant "family leave" for parents of newborns or newly adopted children and for care of elderly or ill family members.
- Promiscuity used to be inhibited by fears of "conception, infection, detection." Infection—especially by herpes and AIDS—still remains a concern, but the others have fallen. The social stigma associated with out-of-wedlock pregnancy has disappeared almost completely.
- We used to live to work; now we work to live.
- Conspicuous consumption is passé; it has been replaced by downscaling.
- Narrow, extremist views of either the left or the right will be unpopular. Moderate Republicans and conservative Democrats will lead their respective parties.
- Some liberal views will be back in the mainstream after 2000, resulting from the thirty-year Hegelian swing in which liberal

and conservative philosophies vie for dominance in American society, eventually reaching stable compromises on most issues.

- Drugs eventually will be decriminalized. The resulting savings from the criminal-justice system will be used for antidrug education and for the treatment of drug users—which will prove to be a more sensible, humane, and effective approach to the problem.

48. Diversity has become a growing, explicit value.

- The old idea was to conform, blend in with the group. This is giving way, especially among minorities, to pride in cultural heritage and a general acceptance of differences in all aspects of society. The interest and acclaim that greeted Alex Haley's *Roots* some years ago is an example. Another is the tolerance, still contested, but growing, for atypical sexual preferences.
- The United States is not a melting pot, but a mosaic. There is strength in the mosaic, but people have different roots, and increasingly they cling to them.
- As the United States grows ethnically more diverse, the reaction among social conservatives and militant extremists will become smaller but more strident.
- This reaction could become particularly acute if economic competition pits older whites against younger blacks, Hispanics, and Asians.

49. Americans place growing importance on economic success, which they have come to expect.

- The emphasis on economic success will remain powerful; stress will keep step with it.
- Growing numbers of people now become entrepreneurs. (See Trend 42.)
- Aspirations are there, but the means to achieve them may

not be. Only one in three high school graduates goes on to receive a college degree.

- Without higher education, expectations may never be met. In 1996, male high school graduates not enrolling in college earned an average of 28 percent less, in constant dollars, than a comparable group in 1973.

- In addition, more young people report no earnings—up from 7 percent of all 20-to-24-year-old men in 1973 to a relatively constant 12 percent since 1984.

50. Tourism, vacationing, and travel (especially international) will continue to grow by about 5 percent per year for the next decade, as it has throughout the 1990s.

- People have more disposable income today, especially in two-earner families.

- The number of Americans traveling to foreign countries (excluding Canada and Mexico) increased at 5 percent per year from 1981 through 1996. Growth will continue at that rate for the foreseeable future.

- International currency exchange rates directly affect travel. Through the beginning of the next century, the dollar will remain comparatively low, compared to other currencies. We therefore can expect more visitors from Europe and Asia.

- By 2001, air travel for both business and pleasure will reach twice the 1985 rate.

- Tourism will benefit as video replaces printed brochures in promoting vacation destinations. Programs include current, detailed information on accommodations, climate, culture, currency, language, immunization, and passport requirements.

- By 2000, one of every ten people in the United States will work for the hospitality industry.

- Multiple, shorter vacations spread throughout the year will continue to replace the traditional two-week vacation.

- More retirees will travel off-season, tending to equalize travel throughout the year and, eliminate the cyclical peaks and valleys typical of the industry.

51. A high level of medical care is increasingly taken for granted.

- Medical knowledge is doubling every eight years.
- As chronic and terminal diseases begin to fade away during the years after 2005 or so, demand for hospital care will decline, while community-based and home care will make up a growing portion of the remaining market.
- More nurses and physical therapists will be available for community-based health care; their salaries will rise.
- Physician assistants will be able to prescribe many drugs in thirty-eight states by 2000. Other drugs, though relatively few, will be reserved for physician prescribers.
- Medical costs will rise at single-digit rates in the early twenty-first century.
- The cost of drugs will increase at roughly the rate of inflation.
- At least seventeen states will authorize druggists to prescribe; only Florida grants this authority now.
- More "surgi-centers," "doc-in-the-boxes," and similar facilities now offer high-quality medical services at the local level. Their share of the health-care market will continue to grow. Home-care and visiting-nurse services will expand even more quickly.
- There will be a surplus of 100,000 physicians by 2001. The result: doctors will pay closer attention to individual patient care and extend their office hours to evenings and weekends. Families will receive much additional medical information via home communication centers. Prescriptions will be written and transmitted via fax or computer.
- After 2005, if today's candidate life-extending therapies prove effective, or 2015 if more sophisticated regimens are required, anti-aging techniques will begin to reduce the rate of chronic disease and will abbreviate terminal illnesses. Thus a decline in the general demand for medical care will

make it easier to provide high-quality care for those who still need it.

52. The physical-culture and personal-health movements will remain strong.

- Emphasis on preventive medicine is growing. By 2001, some 90 percent of insurance carriers will expand coverage or reduce premiums for policyholders with healthy lifestyles.
- Personal wellness, prevention, and self-help will be the watchwords for a more health-conscious population. Interest in participant sports, exercise equipment, home gyms, and employee fitness programs will create mini boom industries.
- Sixty-six percent of those answering a recent Harris poll claimed to have changed their eating habits in the past five years. Americans today eat lighter fare than in 1970, consuming nearly twice as much chicken, over 25 percent more fish, and four times as much low-fat and skim milk per capita.
- Consumer purchases show a per capita decline in annual liquor consumption, from 42.8 gallons in 1980 to 37.4 gallons in 1990. Consumption of distilled liquors has declined, on average, for some two decades, while that of beer and wine accounts for more of the market. Twenty-plus drinkers have revived the once passé taste for mixed drinks, but have proved to be uncommonly responsible drinkers. Most limit themselves to one or two drinks with a meal, and "designated drivers" are standard practice.
- Smoking is also in general decline. Only 29 percent of American men smoke, down from a peak of 50 percent; 23 percent of women smoke, down from 32 percent.
- There are many more magazines on health care and fitness than in the past.
- People will be more inclined to take steps to control stress as they realize that 80 to 90 percent of all diseases are stress-related.
- There are many more nonsmoking areas, smoke-free zones,

and smoke-free restaurants, and their numbers are growing rapidly.

- Life extension will make us still more conscious of our appearance and physical condition. As people get used to the idea of living longer, they will want their extra decades to be as healthy and vigorous as possible. Health clubs continue to boom. Diet, fitness, stress control, and wellness programs will prosper. The tobacco companies could eventually look back on the lawsuit-filled '90s as the good old days.

53. Americans increasingly expect a high level of social service.

- Social Security will require drastic changes in order to remain solvent, if that is possible at all. The program should remain adequate for current pensioners if the retirement age goes to 67 and 70 instead of 62 and 65, though means testing also may be necessary. However, when the Baby Boom generation proves unwilling to die off at a mere 70 or 80 years, the program will be stretched beyond any possible repair. Those not already receiving Social Security income by 2010 very probably never will.
- More services and accommodations have catered to the deaf, blind, disabled, poor, infirm, and aged since the 1992 disabilities act was signed.
- AIDS research and treatment will continue to require funding of nearly $5 billion per year through 2010.
- More psychiatric help will become available for alcohol and drug abuse.
- It is likely to be needed. Though many of us will view the prospect of longer life, or at least of a reprieve from death, as good news, any such dramatic change in our circumstances will require a stressful adjustment that many people will be unable to make without professional help.

54. Concern for environmental issues is growing, especially as Vice President Gore helps President Clinton to build an "environmental administration."

- Life-extended Baby Boomers will return to the activism of their youth, pressing for reassessment of major environmental problems. Topics for attention include air pollution, acid rain, loss of forests, depletion of the ozone layer, global climate change, toxic chemicals in food and water, soil erosion, mass extinction of species, and pollution of beaches, oceans, reservoirs, and waterways.
- Zoos will serve as "Noah's Archives" in an effort to slow the increasing extinction rate of animals.
- Most U.S. cities are quickly filling their existing landfills and will need to develop alternatives for waste disposal. Better recycling and the practice of designing new products to avoid waste have delayed a garbage crisis once expected for the 1990s, but it is difficult to see how a landfill shortage can be avoided for much longer. By 2010, the United States will adopt stringent recycling and waste-reduction mandates already standard in Germany and Japan.
- Warming of the earth's atmosphere caused by the greenhouse effect will result in a worldwide rise in sea levels; national governments will implement policies to require less use of fuels that release carbon dioxide, develop more efficient energy technologies, and combat deforestation.
- A new breed of inherently safe nuclear reactor will take the place of conventional light-water nuclear reactors, which are bound for extinction. They will be small, located underground, and equipped with sealed fuel particles.
- Ocean-wave power plants will produce both electricity and fresh water for island communities. More islands will be inhabited as a result.
- Concern for the indoor environment will increase. New regulations will control the quality of indoor air, the effect of building materials, asbestos, and radon gas.

55. Consumerism is still growing rapidly.

- Consumer agencies and organizations will spread.
- Better information—unit pricing, better content labels,

warning labels, and the like—will proliferate via packaging, TV, and special studies and reports.
- With a wealth of information, much of it supplied by the Internet, consumers will become smarter buyers. They will demand quality, service, dependability, and fair prices.
- Discount stores such as Home Depot and Wal-Mart, factory outlets, and food clubs will continue to grow.

56. The women's equality movement will become less strident, but more effective.

- "Old-girl" networks will become increasingly effective as women fill more positions in middle and upper management.
- Having Boomer women in business an extra few decades will allow the formation of really entrenched old-girl networks, just as Boomer men will form even stronger networks than before.
- An infrastructure is evolving that allows women to make more decisions and to exercise political power, especially where both spouses work. The effect will be:
- more child-care services;
- greater employment opportunities;
- and more equal male-female pay rates. However, the "comparable worth" concept has a future.
- One indication of the growing dependence on the wife's income: Life insurance companies are selling more policies to women than to men.
- More woman are entering the professions, politics, and judicial positions.

FAMILY TRENDS

57. Birthrates are declining.

- The birthrate per 1,000 population has declined from 24.1 in 1950 to 23.7 in 1960, 18.4 in 1970, and 15.9 in 1980. By

1990, it was down to 16.7. Among Generation X parents, it is only 14.3. Between 1970 and 1994, the number of children born each year per 1,000 women age 15 (18, prior to 1990) to 44 has fallen from 87.9 to 67.1. The peak, in 1957, was 122.7!

- Families are getting smaller. In 1991, the average number of people living in a U.S. household was 2.63, down from 3.67 in 1940. Generation X couples almost uniformly say they want two children, no more.

58. Rates of marriage and family formation are inching upward.

- This reverses a long-term trend. The U.S. marriage rate dropped steadily from the 1960s through 1993, when it bottomed at 9.0 marriages per 1,000 people.
- One factor turning the long decline into an increase is the fear of AIDS.
- There will be a surplus of eligible men and a shortage of eligible women in their 20s. The ratio of men to women in this age group in 1973 was 93 to 100, but has been climbing ever since. In 2000, there will be 103 men for every 100 women in their 20s. The result will be a rise in the number of family formations.
- Among older Americans, the proportion of men also has begun to rise, from a minimum of 67.2 men per 100 women over 65 in 1990 to just over 69 per 100 today. By 2010, the ratio will be rising rapidly, as replacements of such hormones as melatonin and DHEA dramatically improve health and lower death rates in later years. This too could spur an increase in marriages.
- Generation Xers are marrying later in life than their parents did, with many delaying marriage until their 30s. One reason is economic. Most say they want to establish their careers and income before building a family.

59. The divorce rate is declining and is likely to continue dropping.

- The long rise in divorce rates peaked at 5.3 per year per 1,000 population in 1981 and has declined steadily ever since. By 1994, it had steadied at 4.6 per 1,000.
- One reason is the fear of AIDS, which has discouraged those considering divorce from returning to the single life.
- Divorce rates will continue to drop through the next decade, thanks to the conservative attitudes of those now in their 20s. Often the children of divorce, most 20-somethings want to be absolutely sure their marriage will last before making that commitment.
- Around 2010, there will be a wave of older-age divorces, as ill-matched couples realize that they will have to endure each other for several extra decades unless they opt out of a bad marriage. They will have the health and energy to act on their dissatisfaction.
- On the other side of the equation, the need for two incomes will still tend to keep people together, and a reaction against the social and cultural changes triggered by life extension probably will extend the fashion for "family values."

60. We will regain our leisure time in the early twenty-first century, and then some.

- Computerized manufacturing—both traditional automation and the newer CAD/CAM and CIM—will result in a shorter average workweek.
- Both spouses working means more disposable income to spend on leisure activities.
- A shorter workweek is coming, at least in major corporations. Sweden is now at thirty-six hours; West Germany is at thirty-seven hours, headed for thirty-five. As more people enter the labor force, the workweek will drop to thirty-two hours, leaving more time for recreation and study.
- Entrepreneurs will be the exception. Their workweek is now over fifty hours and rising.

61. The do-it-yourself movement will continue to grow.

   - The high cost of hiring outside workers motivates people to do the work themselves.
   - There will be more leisure time available to spend on do-it-yourself projects.
   - Availability of more discounted professional tools and supplies for the do-it-yourself market will spur the movement.
   - More videotapes and books are also available for do-it-yourselfers.

62. The nutrition and wellness movements will spread, further improving the health of the elderly.

   - The average child born in 1986 will live to be 74.9 years old—71.5 years for males, 78.5 years for females.
   - Since the beginning of the twentieth century, every generation has lived three years longer than the last, even without anti-aging treatments.

63. Despite popular misconceptions, children are becoming increasingly isolated from the world of adult concern.

   - Many parents overprotect their children from the outside world and the consequences of their acts.
   - Two-income couples are seldom available to discuss adult problems in the children's hearing. Difficult conversations occur after the children are in bed.
   - The exception to this is television, which heightens the impact of news and violence in programs.
   - More children are being placed in day-care centers and preschools. Many are near old-age homes where young and old can share a common bond. These are controlled environments free of many adult worries.
   - As the life-extended population ages, children will come to seem ever more rare and precious. They will be still more

protected, catered to, and generally separated from adult concerns.

64. Adolescence is stretching into early adulthood.

- The median age at first marriage among men has moved from 22.5 in 1970 to 25.8 in 1988 and 26.7 in 1994.
- Women have delayed their first marriage from a median age of 20.6 in 1970 to 23.7 in 1988 and 24.5 in 1994.
- The generation now in their 20s are marrying even later— age 27 or so for men and 25 for women. Nearly 30 percent of men and 20 percent of women still have not married by age 30—respectively double and triple the rates of 1970.

65. Single heads of households are increasingly common. They are the new poor.

- In 1970, only 13 percent of families with children were headed by a single parent. By 1994, the figure was one in three. Nearly 87 percent, or 9.9 million, of such families were headed by the mother.
- The number of households headed by women who never married has exploded from only 248,000 in 1970 to 3.8 million in 1994.
- Because the 20s generation has turned out to be more restrained in their sexual and marital habits than their parents were at the same age, these numbers should remain stable for at least ten years.
- As divorce spreads among the life-extended, we could see a generation of older women living on their own, with few of the skills and resources they need to do so successfully. That implies that we will see a new, previously unanticipated generation in poverty.

66. America's large aged population is growing rapidly.

- Persons age 65 and older made up only 9.8 percent of the American population in 1970. By 2000, they will make up

12.6 percent of the population. The Census Bureau estimates that people of retirement age will make up 13.2 percent of the population in 2010 and 20 percent in 2050. However, these estimates do not account for the coming of extended life spans.

- Persons age 85 and older are now the fastest-growing segment of the American population. As recently as 1970, only 0.7 percent of people were in this age group. By 2000, the number will be 1.6 percent. According to the Census Bureau, it will rise to 1.9 percent in 2010 and 4.6 percent in 2050. Again, this overlooks the coming revolution in aging.

67. Family structures are becoming more diverse.

- In periods of economic difficulty, children and grandchildren move back in with parents and grandparents, to save on living expenses.
- Growing numbers of grandparents are raising their grandchildren, because drugs and AIDS have left the middle generation either unable or unavailable to care for their children.
- Among the poor, grandparents are also providing live-in day care for the children of single mothers trying to gain an education or build a career.
- Yet the nuclear family is also rebounding, as Baby Boom parents adopt "family values" and grandparents retain more independence and mobility.
- Older people remain healthier longer, thanks to better medical care and more healthful lifestyles.
- The older person's family can be near, but not next door.
- Prefabricated (manufactured) housing will be cheaper than conventional construction, enabling older persons to afford housing in the suburbs or wherever they want to live.

INSTITUTIONAL TRENDS

68. As the federal government shrinks, state and local governments are growing.

- The workforce in the federal executive branch has dropped from 3.07 million in 1990 (including part-time and temporary employees) to 2.85 million in 1995.
- In contrast, state and local governments employ more of the workforce. Between 1990 and 1995, their employment rolls have grown from 15.2 million to 16.46 million. Early in the next millennium, state and local governments will provide no less than 85 percent of full-time paid government jobs.
- The decision to replace direct federal spending with bloc grants to state and local governments is one major cause for the change.
- Automation is another. Like industry, government is computerizing the manager's role. The span of control is rising from seven subordinates to fifteen. Middle managers (GS-13 to GS-15) are declining. Federal officials have less direct contact with the public, while state and local governments have more.
- The Clinton administration's "Reinventing Government" plan will reduce federal government workers by 12 percent by 2003, with savings of $120 billion by 2000.

69. Multinational corporations are uniting the world, and growing more exposed to its risks.

- By 2005, parts for well over 50 percent of the products built in the United States will originate in foreign countries.
- Multinational corporations that rely on indigenous workers may be hindered by the increasing number of AIDS cases in Africa and around the world. Up to 90 percent of the population in sub-Saharan Africa reportedly test positive for the HIV virus in some surveys. Thailand is equally stricken, and many other parts of Asia show signs that the AIDS epidemic is spreading among their populations.

70. This international exposure includes a greater risk of terrorist attack.

- The uneasy rapprochement between Israel and its neighbors—the Palestine Liberation Organization, Jordan, Syria, and Lebanon—has eased one major source of terrorist activity.
- State-sponsored terrorism is on the decline, as tougher sanctions make it more trouble than it is worth.
- The new American policy of paying informants to identify terrorists and warn of planned incidents will inhibit violence by the larger, better-established groups.
- However, nothing will prevent small, local political organizations and special-interest groups from using terror to promote their causes. Serb threats to bomb major Western cities in response to any intervention in the Bosnian war are one good example of this.
- On balance, the amount of terrorist activity in the world is likely to go up, not down, in the remainder of the decade.
- The advent of extended life could severely aggravate this problem if the world's poorer regions are not soon integrated into the developed world. The existence of extended life in a world of poverty, disease, and hopelessness will be an invitation to violence.

71. Futures studies and forecasting have become a growth industry.

- Business and government need to know the consequences of expensive or irreversible acts before the decision is taken.
- They also need to anticipate problems that could develop.
- Future-oriented organizations have gained membership and influence steadily since the early 1960s, when they first appeared. The momentum developed in the 1970s can be expected to grow, and such organizations will have increasing influence on decision-making in government, business, and industry in the years ahead.
- A conservative estimate of the number of futurist groups in the world in 1975 and 1976 by the World Future Society was 300; a spokeswoman from the society believes the number of

organizations has increased tremendously in the ensuing years.
- There is a new Congressional Clearinghouse for Futures Research.
- The effects of life extension will cause a boom among futures researchers and keep them busy for many years.

72. American voters increasingly demand accountability in the expenditure of public resources.

- Computers make it easier to keep transaction information (i.e., audit trails), facilitating accountability.
- Concern over the federal budget deficit has fueled demands for greater accountability for waste and fraud in government.
- The public and state legislatures are requiring greater accountability for the outcome of efforts in public education.
- This trend is growing into a general demand that government do its job efficiently and reliably. Life-extended Boomers could be less tolerant of bad government than they are now. After all, they are going to have to put up with any deficiencies a lot longer.
- They will be no more likely to agree about what must be done to improve government than they are today.

73. American consumers increasingly demand social responsibility from companies and each other.

- Union Carbide's Bhopal disaster is a classic case in point.
- Nuclear power plant controversies are now seen in the light of the Chernobyl nuclear accident.
- Safety testing of children's toys also enforces corporate responsibility.
- Auto seat belts and air bags, especially seat-belt-use laws, extend to personal as well as corporate behavior.
- Testing for AIDS and drug abuse carries the demand into intimately personal acts.
- The growing national resolve to attack social problems such

as homelessness, AIDS, drug abuse, and the environment helps fuel this trend.

- Companies will be judged on how they treat the environment.
- Government intervention will supplant deregulation in the airline industry (in the interest of safety and services), financial services (to control instability and costs), electric utilities (nuclear problems), and the chemical industry (toxic wastes).
- With 5 percent of the world's population and 66 percent of the lawyers on the planet, American citizens will not hesitate to litigate if their demands are not met.

74. Institutions are undergoing a bimodal distribution: the big get bigger, the small survive, and the midsized are squeezed out.

- Seven domestic carriers today control 80 percent of the market, leaving the smaller domestic carriers with only 20 percent. By 2001 there will be only three major domestic carriers.
- By 2005, twenty major automakers around the world will hold market shares ranging from 18.1 percent (GM) to 1.0 percent (BMW). By 2010, there will be only five giant automobile firms. Production and assembly will be centered in Korea, Italy, and Latin America.
- By 2000, just three major corporations will make up the computer hardware industry: IBM, Digital, and Apple.
- Manufacturers often sell directly to the dealer, skipping the wholesaler or distributor.
- The 1990s will be the decade of micro-segmentation as more and more highly specialized businesses and entrepreneurs search for narrow niches. These small firms will prosper, even as midsized, "plain vanilla" competitors die out. This trend extends to:
- **Retail.** Big chain department stores and giant discounters succeed. So do small boutiques.
- **Hotels.** Both large, luxurious hotel chains and economy ho-

tels are thriving. Mid-priced family operations are being squeezed out.

- **Restaurants.** Both elegant dining and cheap fast-food restaurants are making it at the expense of sit-down family restaurants.
- **Hospitals.** Large hospital corporations and small walk-in medical centers are flourishing. Single independent hospitals and small chains are being absorbed by the large corporations. (Note that this industry is due for a major contraction when anti-aging therapies are widely adopted.)
- **Agriculture.** The farmer making over $500,000 is flourishing; the farmer who makes under $100,000 is surviving on non-farm income; the middle-income farmer is going bankrupt.
- **Banks.** Interstate and international banks are growing rapidly; at the other end of the spectrum, local banks that emphasize service are succeeding.
- **Financial institutions.** Small, local brokers are prospering, while independents must merge to survive.
- This trend leads us to believe that AT&T may be reconsolidated by 2010.
- Through 2005 to 2010, "boutique" businesses that provide entertainment, financial planning, and preventive medical care for past-their-prime Baby Boomers will be among the fastest-growing segments of the U.S. economy.
- Thereafter, these businesses will either decline (in the case of preventive medicine) or retool themselves to serve a more vigorous and optimistic and much-longer-lived clientele than they had foreseen.

FIFTY TRENDS FOR A POSTMORTAL WORLD

POPULATION

1. In the industrialized countries, the "birth dearth" has cut growth almost to nothing, while in the developing world the population bomb is still exploding.

   - The rich get richer, the poor have children. Throughout the industrialized world, workers can look forward to national retirement programs or social security. In the developing lands, those too old for labor rely on their children to support them—so they have as many as they can.
   - Thanks to better health care, children have a greater chance to survive into adulthood and produce children of their own. This will tend to accelerate population growth, but contraceptive use is increasing, with an opposite effect on growth.
   - In the developed world, the vast Baby Boom generation is approaching middle age, threatening to overwhelm both medical and social security programs. According to the common wisdom, these costs will consume an increasing portion of national budgets until about 2020.
   - In reality, successful age-preventing therapies will dramatically reduce the incidence of heart disease, cancer, and virtually all the other diseases to which the elderly are prone. Ultimately, this will cut overall medical costs in the developed world to much less than half their current levels.
   - At the same time, the addition of forty years or more of ac-

tive life during what once were the retirement years will make it impossible to fund current social security and pension programs. The impossibility of traditional retirement except for the wealthy will be clear as early as 2010, but it will be a decade later before governments and the general populace accept that there is no way to save this tradition, even for those who already have retired.

2. The AIDS epidemic will continue to slaughter millions of people worldwide, especially in Africa and Asia.

    - According to the World Health Organization, the AIDS-causing human immunodeficiency virus will have infected up to 40 million people by 2005.
    - By 2000, some 5 million people in sub-Saharan Africa already will carry the disease—twice as many as a decade earlier. In some cities, as much as 40 percent of the population may be infected.

3. A host of new medical technologies will make life longer and more comfortable in the industrialized world. However, it could be many years before these advances spread to the developing countries.

    - Working independently, two researchers have made important breakthroughs against Alzheimer's disease. One has devised the first specific test for the illness. (Formerly, it was identified largely by eliminating other possible explanations for its symptoms and could be confirmed only on autopsy.) The other reportedly has used surgery to cure some patients of the disorder. If his work pans out, it will banish the single greatest terror of growing old.
    - However, we may not grow old at all. Two scientists appear to have found a way to keep us permanently young, or at least youthful. It seems that loss of stamina, vulnerability to disease, and most other symptoms of aging are due to the

progressive failure of a gland called the pineal. Supplements of melatonin, its natural product, extend the lives of mice by about 25 percent and keep them healthy, active, and young-looking to the end. There is no guarantee that melatonin will prove so effective in human beings, but the discovery clearly foretells the development of a way to prevent aging and extend our life span, very probably within the next decade. Anyone who expected to survive until 2010 or 2015 can reasonably hope for several extra decades of healthy, active life.

- Scientists have discovered that in adults a hormone called human chorionic gonadotropin, or hCG, appears only in cancer cells. Thus antibodies to hCG can reveal the presence of undiagnosed tumors, locate them, and carry cancer-killing drugs to tumors throughout the body. At least one noted cancer specialist not involved with the work forecasts that this will be the long-sought "magic bullet" against cancer.

- Researchers already are testing possible genetic cures for cystic fibrosis, hemophilia, rheumatoid arthritis, familial hypercholesterolemia, AIDS, and no fewer than sixteen different types of cancer. As the Human Genome Project in the United States identifies all of the fifty thousand or more bits of DNA that go to make up a human being, many more such developments will follow. That effort is well ahead of its original schedule.

4. As the West grows ever more concerned with physical culture and personal health, developing countries are adopting the unhealthy practices that wealthier nations are casting off: smoking, high-fat diets, and sedentary lifestyles. To those emerging from poverty, these deadly luxuries are symbols of success.

- In the United States, smokers are kicking the habit. Only 29 percent of American men smoke, down from 52 percent twenty years ago; 23 percent of women smoke, down from a peak of 34 percent.

- However, the developing world continues to smoke more

each year. Even Europe shows little sign of solving this problem.

5. Better nutrition and the "wellness" movement will raise life expectancies.

    *   In developed countries, children born in the 1980s will live to an average age of 70 for males, 77 for females. In developing countries, the average life expectancies will remain stalled at 59 years for males and 61 for females.

FOOD

6. Farmers will continue to harvest more food than the world really needs, but inefficient delivery systems will prevent it from reaching the hungry.

    *   According to the World Bank, some 800 million people are chronically malnourished by UN standards. As the world population grows, that number will rise.

7. The size and number of farms are changing.

    *   In the United States, the family farm is quickly disappearing. Yet giant agribusinesses reap vast profits, while small, part-time "hobby" farms also survive. This trend will eventually spread to the rest of the developed world.
    *   Former Iron Curtain countries are finding it difficult to turn their huge, inefficient collective farms back to private owners. Progress in this effort will continue, but unevenly.
    *   Land reform in Latin America and the Philippines will continue to move at a glacial pace, showing progress only when revolution threatens. Most of the vast holdings now owned by the rich and worked by the poor will survive well into the twenty-first century.

8. According to the authoritative U.S. Office of Technology Assessment (recently disbanded by a Congress that found it inconveniently apolitical), science is continuing to increase the world's food supply.

    • Genetic engineering and other yield-increasing technologies now account for more than 80 percent of the growth in world harvests. The rest comes from newly cultivated croplands.
    • Biotechnology is bringing new protein to developing countries. Bovine growth hormone can produce 20 percent more milk per pound of cattle feed; genetic engineering and cloning are creating both fish that grow faster in aquafarms and crop plants that flourish in arid and salt-contaminated lands.
    • The oceans represent one possible exception to this trend. Evidence suggests that overfishing may have begun to reduce catches in several traditionally important fishing grounds.

9. Food supplies will become more wholesome.

    • Most nations will adopt higher and more uniform standards of hygiene and quality, the better to market their food products internationally. Consumers the world over will benefit.

10. Water will be plentiful in most regions. Total use of water worldwide early in the twenty-first century will be less than half of the stable renewable supply. Yet some parched, populous areas will run short. Most of these have high birthrates, which will aggravate local shortages.

    • The amount of water needed in western Asia has nearly doubled since 1980 and continues to grow. As many as twenty-five nations in Africa and the Middle East already face significant water shortages. The American West also has begun to run short; in some regions, farmers who depended for decades on irrigation have been forced back to arid-land agriculture.

- We already know how to cut water use and waste-water flows by up to 90 percent. Many of these water-saving techniques are being adopted quickly in Japan and Germany, less rapidly in the other industrialized lands. As late as 2005, developing countries still will reuse little of their waste water, because they lack the sewage systems required to collect it. Building this needed infrastructure is becoming a high priority in many parched lands.

- Cheaper, more effective desalination methods are becoming available. In the next twenty years, they will make it easier to live in many desert areas.

ENERGY

11. Despite all the calls to develop alternative sources of energy, oil will continue to provide most of the world's power.

- OPEC will supply most of the oil used in the first decades of the twenty-first century. Demand for OPEC oil grew from 15 million barrels a day in 1986 to over 20 million just three years later. By 2000, it will easily top 25 million barrels per day.

12. Oil prices are not likely to rise. Instead, by 2005 they will plummet to the area of $9 per barrel, where they will remain, with only temporary perturbations, for the foreseeable future.

- Oil is inherently cheap. It costs only $1.50 per barrel to lift Saudi oil out of the ground. Even Prudhoe Bay oil and North Sea oil cost only $6 per barrel.

- The twenty most industrialized countries all have three-month supplies of oil in tankers and storage farms. If OPEC raises its prices too high, its customers can afford to stop

buying until the cost comes down. This was not the case during oil shocks of the 1970s.

13. Growing competition from other energy sources also will help
to hold down the price of oil.

   • Natural gas burns cleanly, and there is enough of it available
     to supply the world's entire energy need for the next 200
     years.
   • Solar, geothermal, wind-generated, and wave-generated
     energy sources will contribute where geographically and
     economically feasible, but their total contribution will be
     small.
   • In Eastern Europe and the nations of the former Soviet
     Union, nuclear plants supply about 12 percent of the energy
     used. In the world as a whole, the figure is only 6.4 percent.
     These numbers will rise during the early twenty-first cen-
     tury as today's relatively primitive reactors are replaced by
     designs that "burn" virtually all of their nuclear fuel and au-
     tomatically shut down if anything goes wrong.
   • Some time later, fusion power finally will come online. Based
     on current work, a commercial-scale prototype reactor could
     enter operation as early as 2015. Commercial energy pro-
     duction would then begin by 2020. Eventually, fusion energy
     will relegate petroleum to its role as a raw material in the
     production of industrial chemicals.

ENVIRONMENT

14. Air pollution and other atmospheric issues will dominate
ecopolicy discussions for years to come.

   • Soot and other particulates are being more carefully scruti-
     nized. Evidence shows that they are far more dangerous than
     sulfur dioxide and other gaseous pollutants formerly be-

lieved to present major health risks. In the United States alone, medical researchers estimate that as many as 60,000 people may die each year as a direct result of breathing particulates. Most are elderly and already suffer from respiratory distress.

- By 1985, the concentration of carbon dioxide in the atmosphere was 25 times greater than in preindustrial days. By 2050, the concentration is likely to increase 40 percent over current levels if energy use continues to grow at its current pace. Burning fossil fuel will spew about 7 billion tons of carbon into the air each year by 2000, 10 to 14 billion tons in 2030, and 13 to 23 billion tons in 2050.

- At its annual minimum, the ozone layer over the Antarctic is virtually absent, while the "hole" over the Arctic has begun to spread to populated regions in North America. The resulting excess of ultraviolet radiation reaching Earth's surface already is believed to be changing the Antarctic ecosystem. Even if chlorine compounds responsible for ozone depletion were completely eliminated, it would take nature decades to restore the protective ozone layer.

- Blame global warming for at least some of the spread of Africa's deserts. Before the process runs its course, two-fifths of Africa's remaining fertile land could become arid wasteland. Up to one-third of Asia's nondesert land and one-fifth of Latin America's may follow. Global warming will not only hurt agriculture, but also raise sea levels, with consequent impacts on habitation patterns and industries.

- Brazil and other nations will soon halt the irrevocable destruction of Earth's rain forests for very temporary economic gain. Those countries will need economic help to make the transition. The World Bank and the International Monetary Fund will help underwrite alternatives to rain-forest destruction.

- Acid rain, now coming under control in the United States and Canada, will appear whenever designers of new power plants and factories neglect emission-control equipment. Watch for it in most developing countries.

15. Disposal of mankind's trash is a growing problem, especially in the developed nations. Within the next decade, most of the industrialized world will run out of convenient space in its landfills.

   • This deadline already has been set back by nearly a decade, thanks to better recycling technologies and to efforts to design waste materials out of the production/consumption cycle.
   • By 2005, recycling will become efficient enough to provide some industrial materials more cheaply than producing them from raw precursors. Recycling will save energy as well, since remanufacturing requires less energy than the full iron-ore-to-Cadillac production process.

SCIENCE AND TECHNOLOGY

16. High technological turnover rates are accelerating.

   • All the technological knowledge we work with today will represent only 1 percent of the knowledge that will be available in 2050.
   • Fully 80 percent of all the scientists, physicians, and technicians who have ever lived are alive and working today. Rather than having to rely on letters and printed journals, they are exchanging their ideas and discoveries in near-real time over the Internet.

17. Technology has come to dominate the economy and society in the developed world. Its central role can only grow.

   • For some economists, the number of cars, computers, telephones, facsimile machines, copiers, and Internet connections in a nation define how "developed" the country is.
   • Personal robots will appear in homes by about 2005. Robots will perform mundane commercial and service jobs and en-

vironmentally dangerous tasks, such as repairing nuclear facilities, underwater cables, and the components of orbiting
space stations.

18. The technology gap between developed and developing countries will continue to widen.

 • Developed countries have ten times as many scientists and
   engineers per capita as the developing world. The gap between their spending on research and development grew
   fourfold from 1980 to 1990.
 • Technologically underdeveloped countries face antiquated
   or nonexistent production facilities, a dearth of useful
   knowledge, ineffective organization and management, and a
   lack of technical skills. Under these conditions, underdevel-
   opment often is self-perpetuating. This weakens the country's ability to compete in international markets.
 • The widening technology gap will aggravate the disparity in
   north-south trade, with the developed nations of the northern hemisphere supplying more and more high-tech goods.
   The less developed countries of the southern hemisphere
   will be restricted to exporting natural resources and relatively unprofitable low-tech manufactured products.

19. Nations will exchange scientific data more freely, but will continue to hold back technological information. However, as the
product-development cycle shrinks, the distinction between
basic science and technology is beginning to blur.

 • Basic research is done principally in universities, which have
   a tradition of communicating their findings.
 • Technological discoveries, in contrast, often spring from corporate laboratories, whose sponsors have a keen interest in
   keeping them proprietary. More than half of the technology
   transferred between countries will move between giant corporations and their overseas branches or as part of joint ventures by multinationals and foreign partners.

- Financially strapped universities have begun to carry out much of their research under contract to industry. When this occurs, the corporate wish for secrecy often wins out over the academic tradition of openness. This trend will spread throughout the academic world in the next twenty years.
- Over half of the Ph.D. candidates in U.S. science and engineering programs are from other countries. Anything they learn will return to their homelands when they do.
- The space-faring nations—soon to include Japan—will share their findings more freely.

20. Research and development will play an ever-greater role in the world economy.

- R&D outlays in the United States have varied narrowly (between 2.1 percent and 2.8 percent of the GNP) since 1960 and have been rising generally since 1978.
- R&D spending is growing most rapidly in the electronics, aerospace, pharmaceuticals, and chemical industry.
- Though the United States has traditionally led in R&D spending, which partially accounts for its technological supremacy, other nations are taking the lead. The top three Japanese automakers each spend more for research each year than the entire budget of the U.S. National Science Foundation.

COMMUNICATIONS

21. Communications and information are the lifeblood of a world economy. Thus, the world's communications networks will grow ever more rapidly until both communications satellites and high-speed fiber-optic data lines blanket the globe.

- Already, a person anywhere in the world can send a fax or e-mail from a laptop computer via communications satellite and Internet to anyone in the world who is equipped to receive it.

- By 2005, the Internet's main trunk lines will be at least ten times faster than they are today, while fiber-optic lines will carry data between the major cities of the United States, Europe, and Japan.
- At least five competing networks of communications satellites are planned to enter operation by 2010.

22. The growing power and versatility of computers, combined with access to the Internet, will continue to change the way individuals, companies, and nations do business.

- Processing power and operating speeds for computers are still increasing. By 2005, the average personal computer will have at least a hundred times the power of the first IBM PCs and a thousand or more times the power of the original Apple II.
- Computers and communications are quickly finding their way into information synthesis and decision-making. Voice-recognition software already makes it practical for computers to transcribe dictation in some limited-vocabulary situations. Computers also translate documents from one language to another. Today's best translation programs already can handle a 30,000-word vocabulary in nine languages. By 2010, the world's telephone systems will translate conversations in real time between English, French, German, and Japanese.
- The revolution in computers and communications technologies offers hope that developing countries can catch up with the developed world. Two early beneficiaries are India and Pakistan, which now supply data-keyboarding services for most of the English-speaking world. Few other developing lands have yet been able to profit from the new age of information. In 1995, developing countries owned only 6 percent of the world's computers. Most are used mainly for

accounting, payroll processing, and similar low-payoff operations.

LABOR

23. The world's labor force will grow by only 1.5 percent per year during the next decade—much slower than through much of the late twentieth century, but fast enough to provide most countries with the workers they need. In contrast, the United States faces shortages of labor in general and especially of low-wage-rate workers.

   • Multinational companies that rely on indigenous workers may find their operations handicapped by loss of employees and potential workers to the worldwide epidemic of AIDS, especially in Africa and Asia.

24. The shrinking supply of young workers in many countries means that the overall labor force is aging rapidly.

   • Persons aged 25 to 59 have accounted for 65 percent of the world labor force in recent years. Almost all growth of the labor force over the next decade will occur in this age group.

25. Unions will continue to lose their hold on labor.

   • Union membership is declining in the United States. It was 17.5 percent in 1986 and 16.1 percent in 1990. By 2005, it will fall to less than 12 percent.
   • Unionization in Latin America and Europe will remain about the same as it is today. Union membership in the Pacific Rim will remain low. Unionization in the developing world as a whole will remain extremely low.
   • Increased use of robots, CAD/CAM, and flexible manufac-

turing complexes can cut a company's workforce by up to one-third.

- Growing use of artificial intelligence, which improves productivity and quality, will make the companies adopting it more competitive, but will further reduce the need for workers in the highly unionized manufacturing industries.

26. People will change residences, jobs, and even occupations more frequently, especially in industrialized countries.

- By 2010, high-speed trains like the French TGV will allow daily commutes of up to 500 miles, even in the United States, which has been slow to restore its mass transportation system.
- The number of people who retrain for new careers, one measure of occupational mobility, has been increasing steadily.
- The new information-based organizational management methods—nonhierarchical, organic systems that can respond quickly to environmental changes—foster greater occupational flexibility and autonomy.

27. The wave of new entrepreneurs in the United States during the last twenty years is just the leading edge of a much broader trend. Throughout the developed world, the twenty-something Generation X—skeptical of all institutions, including would-be employers—is proving to be the most entrepreneurial in history. At the same time, older workers displaced by downsizing and outsourcing are building their own companies, rather than seeking new jobs that rarely pay as well as their old ones. When Baby Boomers discover that traditional retirement is all but impossible for people who will live decades longer than they once expected, many more will opt to start their own businesses, rather than go on, or go back to, working for others.

- Since 1983, the number of new businesses started in the United States has remained continuously over 600,000 per year. In 1995, the figure hit a record 750,000. By comparison, in 1950, there were fewer than 100,000 new business incorporations.

- Businesses with fewer than 100 workers now employ some 56 percent of the American labor force; those with fewer than 500 workers employ 80 percent of the labor force. Since the late 1980s, virtually all growth in employment has occurred in small business. Employment by large corporations has remained flat or has declined. In 1995, small businesses generated more than 1 million new full-time jobs, compared with roughly 100,000 generated by larger companies.

- Though figures are harder to come by, this same trend has clearly begun to sweep the rest of the world. In Western Europe, where would-be entrepreneurs were until recently viewed with suspicion, business start-ups are beginning to flower. A new generation of entrepreneurs is growing throughout Eastern Europe, where capitalism has been unleashed after decades of suppression. China and Vietnam increasingly are promoting entrepreneurism. Even in Japan, where culture and tradition discourage individualism, the new generation of businesspeople are beginning to create small, fast-growing enterprises.

28. More women will continue to enter the labor force.

- In both the developed and developing regions, the percentage of working women has increased in recent decades. Women represented some 40 percent of the world's labor force in 1995. This growth is expected to continue at a moderate rate, with developed nations showing the fastest increases.

INDUSTRY

29. Multinational and international corporations will continue to grow, and many new ones will appear.

- Companies will continue to expand, join, and cooperate beyond national borders. For example, in the aerospace industry alone, Lockheed Martin (in the United States) and Krunichev Enterprises and NPO Energia (both Russian) have joined forces to market launch space on the Proton and the Atlas boosters; Aerojet has contracted to buy Russian NK-33 engines and may license the design for production in the United States; Pratt & Whitney is selling Russian rocket engines; and Sea Launch Co. LDC is a collaboration between the American Boeing Commercial Space, Russia's RSC-Energia, NPO-Yuzhnoye in Ukraine, and Kvaerner a.s., a Norwegian shipbuilding giant.
- Many other companies are going international by locating new facilities in countries that provide a labor force and benefits such as preferential tax treatment, but that do not otherwise participate in the operation. Ireland pioneered this practice with U.S. companies in the insurance, electronics, and automobile industries. It found that when companies leave, for whatever reason, the country loses revenue and gains an unemployed labor force. Recently, India, Pakistan, and other countries have followed Ireland's example.

30. Demands will grow for industries to increase their social responsibility.

- A wide variety of environmental disasters and public-health issues (e.g., the *Exxon Valdez* oil spill and Union Carbide's release of toxic gas at Bhopal, India), have drawn public attention to the effects of corporate negligence and to situations in which business can help solve public problems not necessarily of their own making.
- In the future, companies will increasingly be judged on how they treat the environment—and will be forced to clean up any damage resulting from their activities.
- Deregulation will be a thing of the past. There will be increased government intervention. Airlines are being compelled to provide greater safety and services, the financial-

service industry will be regulated to reduce economic instability and costs, electric utilities will be held responsible for nuclear problems, and chemical manufacturers are having to cope with their own toxic wastes.

31. The early twenty-first century will be a time of microsegmentation, as more and more highly specialized businesses and entrepreneurs search for narrower niches in which to prosper.

   - This trend appeared in the early 1990s, when displaced executives increasingly chose to build their own businesses rather than search for jobs that were not to be found.
   - Age-extended executives will follow this trend, either starting post-retirement businesses rather than returning to the job market when their nest egg runs short or moving directly from a previous career to self-employment.

EDUCATION AND TRAINING

32. Literacy will become a fundamental goal in developing societies, and the developed world will take steps to guard against backsliding toward illiteracy. Throughout the world, education (especially primary-school literacy) remains a major goal for development as well as a means of meeting goals for health, higher labor productivity, stronger economic growth, and social integration. Countries with a high proportion of illiterates will not be able to cope with modern technology or use advanced agricultural techniques.

   - Most developed countries have literacy rates of more than 95 percent. The increasing levels of technological "savvy" demanded by modern life, however, often are more than people are prepared to meet, even in the most modern societies.
   - Although their absolute numbers continue to grow, illiterates represent a steadily decreasing proportion of the world's adult population. In developing countries, the number of il-

literates will grow by 5 million during the last five years of the century, but they will have dropped from 34 percent of the adult population in 1995 to 28 percent in 2000.

- Worldwide, the proportion of children not enrolled in school is falling steadily from 21 percent in 1995 and should reach 18 percent by 2000. In the United States, the Goals 2000 program is bringing significant increases in school attendance. Elsewhere, primary-education enrollment has risen dramatically in most of the developing world, except for Africa. In thirty-one sub-Saharan countries reporting their enrollment rates, the rates had fallen for boys in thirteen countries and for girls in fifteen.
- Useful, job-oriented knowledge is becoming increasingly perishable. The half-life of an engineer's professional information today is five years.

33. Educational reform is changing America's schools. In the long run, this will repair the nation's competitive position in the world economy.

- The information economy's need for skilled workers requires more effective schools.
- Science and engineering schools are actively recruiting more students.
- Foreign-exchange programs are growing quickly in an attempt to bolster the competence of American students in international affairs.

34. Higher education is changing as quickly as primary and secondary schools.

- The soaring cost of higher education is beginning to force program cuts. As a result, developing countries may face an ultimate loss of foreign exchange, as their industries fall farther behind those of more efficient competitors.
- There are too few jobs for liberal-arts graduates in many de-

veloping countries. For example, Egypt has failed to keep its promise to give a job to every graduate; the civil service is grossly overstaffed already. Young, educated, but unemployed men are becoming a source of political instability throughout the Middle East.

- The concept of a "university" is changing. Increasingly, major corporations are collaborating with universities to establish degree-granting corporate schools and programs. Examples include the General Motors Institute, Motorola University, Pennsylvania State University's affiliation with a major electronics company, and Rutgers University's affiliation with a major pharmaceuticals house.

- Over the Internet, educational institutions can provide a college degree for one-tenth the cost of attending a public university or one-fifteenth the cost of attending a private school.

- Private companies are marketing large electronic databases, either on CD-ROM or through network access. These products may eventually replace university libraries.

WORLD ECONOMY

35. The world economy will grow at a rapid rate for the foreseeable future, but the gap between the rich and poor countries will widen.

- World trade will grow at a brisk 4.5 percent annually in the next decade. As one result, international competition will continue to cost jobs and income in the developed market economies.

- The Gross Domestic Products of the developed market economies will grow at 3.1 percent, on average, in the late 1990s as investment demand increases and the economic integration in Europe introduces capital efficiency.

- The economies of Eastern Europe and Russia may recover with a GDP growth rate of 3.6 percent.

- The developing economies will fall farther and farther behind the industrialized nations, largely because their populations will continue to rise faster than their incomes. GDPs in the developing economies will grow by 4.3 percent per year (well below the 5.1 percent rate they enjoyed in the 1970s). In the 1970s, their per capita GDP was one-tenth that of the developed countries. By 1995, it had fallen to one-thirteenth. By 2000, it will be one-fourteenth.
- By reducing military budgets, the fabled "new world order" is making more money available for business.

36. The world economy will become increasingly integrated.

- There is a "ripple effect" among closely linked national stock exchanges. The impact of a major event on one exchange perturbs all the others. Stock markets will become more fully connected and integrated.
- By 2000 or so, all national currencies will be convertible, following a model similar to the European Community's Exchange Rate Mechanism.
- It will become increasingly difficult to label a product by nation (e.g., "Japanese cars"), since parts will often come from several countries to be assembled in others and sold in yet others. Protective tariffs will become obsolete—for the good of the worldwide economy.

37. The world is quickly dividing into three major blocks: the European Community, the North American Free Trade Zone, and Asia's informal but very real Pacific development area. Other regions will ally themselves with these giants: Eastern Europe with the EC, Latin America with the United States, Canada, and Mexico. Australia and New Zealand are still trying to make up their minds which of these units to join—the Pacific Rim, where their nearest markets are, or Europe and North America, where their cultural bonds are strongest. It appears that economics will win out over emotion, and they will join the Pacific Rim trading group.

- The economic structure of all these regions is changing rapidly. All but the least developed nations are moving out of agriculture. Service sectors are growing rapidly in the mature economies, while manufacturing is being transferred to the world's developing economies.
- Within the new economic blocs, multinational corporations will not replace the nation-state, but they will become far more powerful, especially as governments relinquish aspects of social responsibility to employers.

38. The European Community will become a major player in the world economy.

- By 2000, the EC will represent a population of 325 million people with a $4 trillion GDP.
- By 2000, the European Free Trade Association countries will join with the EC to create a market of 400 million people with a $5 trillion GDP. Sweden, Norway, Finland, Austria, and Switzerland will join the founding twelve.
- By 2005, most of the former Eastern Bloc countries will be associate members of the EC.

39. The twenty-five most industrialized countries will devote between 1 percent and 2 percent of their GDP to help their poorer neighbors.

- Much aid to poorer countries will be money that formerly would have gone to pay military budgets.
- The World Bank and the International Monetary Fund will help distribute funds.
- Loans and grants may require developing nations to set up population-control programs.

40. Western bankers will at last accept the obvious truth: many Third World debtors have no hope of ever paying back overdue loans. Creditors will thus forgive one-third of these debts. This

will save some of the developing nations from bankruptcy and probable dictatorship.

41. Developing nations once nationalized plants and industries when they became desperate to pay their debts. In the future, the World Bank and the IMF will refuse to lend to nations that take this easy way out. (Debtors, such as Peru, are eager to make amends to these organizations.) Instead, indebted nations will promote private industry in the hope of raising needed income.

42. Washington, D.C., will supplant New York as the world financial capital. The stock exchanges and other financial institutions, especially those involved with international transactions, will move south to be near Congress, the World Bank, and key regulatory bodies.

   • Among the key economic players already in Washington: the Federal Reserve Board, the embassies and commercial/cultural attachés of nearly every country in the world, and the headquarters of many multinational and international corporations.
   • In addition, several agencies cooperating with the United Nations, including the International Monetary Fund and the General Agreement on Tariffs and Trade, have their headquarters in or routinely conduct much of their business in Washington.

WARFARE

43. The world has been made "safer" for local or regional conflicts. During the Cold War, the superpowers could restrain their aggressive junior allies from attacking their neighbors. With the nuclear threat effectively gone, potential antagonists feel less inhibited. Iraqi President Saddam Hussein was only the first of many small despots who will try to win by conquest what cannot be achieved by negotiation.

- The United States and the states of the former Soviet Union have signed a long procession of arms treaties. The United States and Russia will make a virtue of necessity, but both will sign future treaties primarily to cut expensive military programs from their budgets.
- Terrorist states will continue to harbor chemical and biological weapons until the international community finally takes a firm stand.

44. Brushfire wars will grow more frequent and bloody. Among the most likely are:

- Israel vs. its Arab neighbors. We foresee one last generalized conflict in this region before the peace that once seemed near actually becomes a reality. Israel will win this one, too.
- India vs. Pakistan. The two have feuded with each other since the British left in 1947; religious differences, separatism in Kashmir, and small stocks of nuclear weapons make this a hot spot to watch carefully.
- Northern Ireland vs. itself. This perpetually troubled land will remain its own worst enemy. In trying to keep Ireland under control, the British face an increasingly unpleasant task.
- The fundamentalist Islamic lands vs. their more moderate neighbors. The Islamist regimes in Iran and Afghanistan are promoting, and sometimes covertly waging, war against secular governments in nearby Muslim regions of China, the former Soviet Union, and even Eastern Europe. The Chechnyan separatist movement is one such conflict. Any future outbreak of hostilities in Bosnia is likely to be another.

45. Tactical alliances formed by common interests to meet immediate needs will replace long-term commitments among nations.

- In the Middle East, "the enemy of your enemy is your friend." Iran and Iraq will tolerate each other in their stronger

hatred for the West. The United States and Syria will never be
friends, but both dislike Iraq.

- Turkey and Greece will be hard pressed to overlook their differences about Cyprus, but may do so in an effort to counter
terrorism.

INTERNATIONAL ALIGNMENTS

46. The Information Revolution has enabled many people formerly
insulated from outside influences to compare their lives with
those of people in other countries. This knowledge has often
raised their expectations, and citizens in many undeveloped and
repressed lands have begun to demand change. This trend can
only spread as world telecommunications networks become
ever more tightly linked.

   - East Germans learned of reforms elsewhere in Eastern Europe via West German television; Romanians learned
   through Hungarian media.
   - International broadcasting entities such as the Voice of
   America, the British Broadcasting Corporation, ITV, and
   Cable News Network disseminate information around the
   world, sometimes influencing and inspiring global events
   even as they report on them.

47. Politically, the world's most important trend is for nations to
form loose confederations, either by breaking up the most cen-
tralized nations into semiautonomous ethnic and religious regions or by uniting independent countries in international
alliances.

   - Quebec will secede from Canada, probably in 2002 or 2003.
   The four eastern Canadian provinces will be absorbed into
   the United States a year or two later, and the other Canadian
   provinces will follow suit by 2010.
   - When Britain's lease ran out in mid-1997, Hong Kong be-

came the first semiindependent territory to rejoin mainland China. Macao, leased to Portugal, soon will follow. If the capitalist system and political freedoms of these regions are not too seriously abridged, Taiwan will seek to join mainland China within the next five years. The two Koreas now seem bound to reunite as well.

48. The role of major international organizations will become extremely important in the early twenty-first century.

- A smaller, more efficient, and fully funded United Nations will finally be able to carry out its mission. The World Court will enjoy increased prestige. UNESCO's food, literacy, and children's-health funds will be bolstered. The World Health Organization will make progress in disease eradication and in training programs. The Food and Agriculture Organization will receive more funding for starvation relief and programs to help teach farming methods.
- More countries will be willing to reform internally to meet requirements for International Monetary Fund loans and World Bank programs that provide development and education funds and grants.
- More medical aid from developed countries will be provided, frequently under the auspices or coordination of the United Nations or Red Cross/Red Crescent, to countries devastated by plague, famine, or other natural disasters. The Red Cross and Red Crescent will step up their activities in such areas as natural-disaster relief, blood programs, and caring for political prisoners and prisoners of war around the world. They already have assumed these roles in Zaire, Rwanda, Peru, and other lands.
- Cooperation will develop among intelligence agencies from different countries (e.g., Interpol, the CIA, and what remains of the KGB) in order to monitor terrorism and control antiterrorism programs and to coordinate crime fighting worldwide.

49. International bodies will take over much of the peacekeeping role now being abandoned by the superpowers. The Conference on Security and Cooperation in Europe (CSCE)—a group of thirty-five nations (including the United States and Russia)—will pick up where NATO and the Warsaw Pact left off by creating a pan-European security structure.

   • The methods of operation for voting on CSCE matters will likely be revised; currently, each of the member nations holds veto power.

50. The field of public diplomacy will grow, spurred by advances in communication and by the increased importance and power of international organizations.

AGING BY THE NUMBERS

As we finished writing this book, *The Washington Post* (June 1, 1997) published one of the best discussions of modern aging that we have yet seen. In it, writer Susan Cohen surveyed the dramatic ways in which older life has changed, even before the anti-aging revolution takes hold. They are many and important.

"Throughout ninety-nine percent of human history, life expectancy's been under eighteen," points out Ken Dychtwald, a corporate consultant who specializes in issues of the aging. "So what we see happening, literally as we talk, is an evolutionary event—the movement of the human species from being short-lived to long-lived. There has never been a vast generation of middle-aged people concerned with the care of their parents—ever. There has never been a mass generation of people wondering what they're going to do with eighty or ninety years of life—ever."

Dychtwald sees whole new stages appearing in the modern life span. Not long ago children grew to adulthood, progressed clearly into their middle years, and then entered old age. Now, he says, middle age has become divided into at least two stages, neither of which closely resembles the traditional version. In "middlescence," people may retire, build a new career, seek out part-time work, remarry, or all of the above. In "late adulthood," they begin to slow down. Yet, health permitting, and it often does, all of their options remain open to them. "I think we live in an era now where it's become increasingly normal, acceptable, almost institutionalized, for people to have second careers or second marriages." Only in their late seventies and eighties do today's healthy seniors enter old age, the final stage of growing disability and preparation for death.

We, of course, suspect that the change soon to come will be far greater than anything even Dychtwald has imagined. Yet his comments and Cohen's other observations offer useful insights into the transition period, the next ten or twenty years, when people who grow old before life-extending treatments become available will require increasing amounts of social support and medical care. This is a demand with which the United States in particular has yet to come to grips. There are only 7,000 geriatric physicians in the United States today, Cohen points out. The Alliance for Aging Research estimates that the country needs at least 16,000. It will need many more than that before this final wave of traditional aging has passed.

Many key facts about aging as we currently experience it are summarized in the tables below. The data come from surveys conducted by Belden & Rusonello for the Alliance for Aging Research; from *Washington Post* national surveys; from the General Social Survey conducted by the National Opinion Research Center at the University of Chicago; and from the AHEAD Survey, with data analyzed by Beth Soldo, of Georgetown University. The tables were prepared by Richard Morin, director of polling for *The Washington Post*.

ON AGING

Americans under the age of 65 seemingly can't wait to get old. Asked in a recent national survey whether they expected the following to improve, get worse, or stay the same after age 65, they replied:

	WILL IMPROVE	GET WORSE	STAY THE SAME
Your financial security	55%	13%	31%
Your enjoyment of life	55	4	39
Feeling personally fulfilled	52	5	43
Relationship with your spouse or companion	50	3	38
Your religious or spiritual faith	49	1	46
Relationships with your children	46	2	36

Your relationships with friends	38	3	57
Your sex life	31	16	48
Your physical health	22	33	44
Your physical appearance	20	41	37

Not so fast, say those on the other side of 65. Now that they've gotten there, they see things differently. Here's what they said has happened to them since their 65th birthday:

	IMPROVED	WORSENED	STAYED THE SAME
Your financial security	19%	17%	63%
Your enjoyment of life	26	14	56
Feeling personally fulfilled	24	7	65
Relationship with your spouse or companion	22	3	47
Your religious or spiritual faith	29	1	70
Relationships with your children	19	2	73
Your relationships with friends	23	3	73
Your sex life	6	16	51
Your physical health	10	32	58
Your physical appearance	10	20	66

Note: Rows may not total to 100 because percentage with no opinion is not shown.

WORST FEARS

Americans aren't afraid to die, but they do fear that life may not be worth living when they're old. Here's the proportion who said they were worried about:

Living for many years in a nursing home because of physical frailty or long-term illness	64%
Developing Alzheimer's disease	56
Becoming a financial burden on their children or other people	47
Being lonely	36
Loss of physical attractiveness	34
Death	28
Having nothing to do	26

INDEPENDENCE DAYS

Is it a good idea or a bad idea for older parents to move in with their adult children? The opposition comes from a surprising age group.

	Good Idea	Bad Idea	Depends
18–34	57%	29%	14%
35–64	51	32	17
65 or older	19	61	20

WEARING OUT

Few older Americans have escaped the physical effects of aging. Here's the percentage of Americans 70 or older who:

Have a major chronic disease	80%
Are frail and need help to function	36
Have cognitive problems	36
Are in excellent physical, emotional, and cognitive health	16

MONEY MATTERS

Financially speaking, the golden years may not be that golden. But older Americans aren't complaining. Here's how younger, middle-aged, and older people assessed their present financial condition:

	Satisfied	More or Less Satisfied	Not Satisfied
18–34	21%	48%	31
35–64	27	45	28
65 or older	44	44	12

THE CENTURY MARK

As life spans have extended, Americans have raised their sights. Here's the percentage of each group who said they'd like to live to be 100.

Men	66%
Women	56
Whites	60
Blacks	78
18–31	68
32–50	62
51–64	59
65 and older	53

INDEX